THE COLLEGE PRESS NIV COMMENTARY

JAMES & JUDE

THE COLLEGE PRESS NIV COMMENTARY

JAMES & JUDE

GARY HOLLOWAY

New Testament Series Co-Editors:

Jack Cottrell, Ph.D.
Cincinnati Bible Seminary

Tony Ash, Ph.D.
Abilene Christian University

COLLEGE PRESS
PUBLISHING COMPANY
Joplin, Missouri

Copyright © 1996
College Press Publishing Company

All Scripture quotations, unless indicated, are taken from
THE HOLY BIBLE: NEW INTERNATIONAL VERSION®.
Copyright © 1973, 1978, 1984 by International Bible Society.
Used by permission of Zondervan Publishing House.
All rights reserved.

The "NIV" and "New International Version" trademarks are registered in the United States Patent and Trademark Office by International Bible Society. Use of either trademark requires the permission of International Bible Society.

Printed and Bound in the
United States of America
All Rights Reserved

Library of Congress Cataloging-in-Publication Data

Holloway, Gary, 1956–
   James and Jude / Gary Holloway.
     p. cm. – (The College Press NIV commentary)
   Includes bibliographic references.
   ISBN 0-89900-638-8
   1. Bible. N.T. James—Commentaries. 2. Bible. N.T. Jude—
  Commentaries. I. Title. II. Series.
BS2785.3.H65 1996
227'.91077—dc20   96-19725
                                                                                CIP

A WORD FROM THE PUBLISHER

Years ago a movement was begun with the dream of uniting all Christians on the basis of a common purpose (world evangelism) under a common authority (The Word of God). The College Press NIV Commentary Series is a serious effort to join the scholarship of two branches of this unity movement so as to speak with one voice concerning the Word of God. Our desire is to provide a resource for your study of the New Testament that will benefit you whether you are preparing a Bible School lesson, a sermon, a college course or your own personal devotions. Today as we survey the wreckage of a broken world, we must turn again to the Lord and his Word, unite under his banner and communicate the life-giving message to those who are in desperate need. This is our purpose.

FOREWORD

I owe a debt of gratitude to many for assistance with this volume. John York and John Hunter are responsible for making me a part of the *College Press NIV Commentary* project. The Institute for Christian Studies, Austin, Texas, allowed me a sabbatical to complete this project. St. Deiniol's Library, Hawarden, Wales, afforded me a generous scholarship to use their considerable resources during my sabbatical. I particularly appreciate the advice and encouragement of my colleague, Jeff Peterson. Most of all, I thank my wife, Deb, for her helpful comments on the manuscript and her constant good humor.

My prayer is that this volume will guide you to a fuller understanding of James and Jude and through them to a closer walk with Jesus, their brother and ours.

ABBREVIATIONS

BAGD .... *Bauer-Arndt-Gingrich-Danker Greek Lexicon (2nd. ed.)*
DSB .... *Daily Study Bible*
ICC .... *International Critical Commentary*
JBL .... *Journal of Biblical Literature*
JETS .... *Journal of the Evangelical Theological Society*
JSNT .... *Journal for the Study of the New Testament*
KJV .... *King James Version*
LWC .... *Living Word Commentary*
LXX .... *Septuagint*
MNTC .... *Moffatt New Testament Commentary*
NAC .... *New American Commentary*
NCB .... *New Clarendon Bible*
NCBC .... *New Century Bible Commentary*
NEB .... *New English Bible*
NIBC .... *New International Bible Commentary*
NIGTC .... *New International Greek Testament Commentary*
NRSV .... *New Revised Standard Version*
NTC .... *New Testament Commentary*
NTS .... *New Testament Studies*
PNTC .... *Pelican New Testament Commentary*
REB .... *Revised English Bible*
RSV .... *Revised Standard Version*
TBC .... *Torch Bible Commentaries*
TDNT .... *Theological Dictionary of the New Testament, ed. by Gerhard Kittel and Gerhard Friedrich*
TEV .... *Today's English Version*

THE BOOK OF
JAMES

INTRODUCTION

My first introduction to the book of James was in a Bible class at a Christian school my sophomore year of high school. For much of the school year we studied James. The next year, the Bible curriculum was changed, new teachers were hired, and somehow we ended up studying James again. It is a compliment to the power of the book of James that I was not discouraged by that double introduction. Instead, I found the book interesting and challenging both years. Since then James has profoundly shaped my preaching, teaching, and my Christian walk. The book of James is maligned by some and neglected by many. My prayer is that this commentary will help others discover the call to radical discipleship, to rejection of the values of the world, and to friendship with God made by this faithful leader in the apostolic age.

AUTHORSHIP

The writer identifies himself as "James, a servant of God and of the Lord Jesus Christ" (James 1:1). The name "James" (Greek *Iakobos*) comes from the Hebrew name "Jacob." It was a popular name for Hebrew men, recalling the rich heritage of Jacob, the founder of Israel. There are five persons named James in the New Testament who could have written this letter.

1. James the brother of Jesus. Some think this is the same James as the son of Alphaeus or "the less" (see below), but that is unlikely.

2. James the apostle, the son of Zebedee. Not only was he

an apostle but (along with Peter and John) was part of the inner circle of Jesus who witnessed the Transfiguration and the agony in Gethsemane. However, this James was beheaded by Herod Agrippa I around A.D. 44 (Acts 12:2), making it unlikely he wrote the letter (unless it is by far the earliest New Testament book). Also, if this James wrote the letter, it is strange he did not call himself "an apostle" but only "a servant."

3. James the apostle, the son of Alphaeus (Matthew 10:3; Acts 1:13). The same objection, the author does not call himself an apostle, applies here. Although this James was an apostle, little is known about him.

4. James "the less" (or "the younger," Mark 15:40). Little is known of this James also, making it unlikely that he would write a letter accepted as authoritative. This may be the same James as #3.

5. James, the father of Judas (Luke 6:16; Acts 1:13). He too is obscure.

There are two other possibilities for authorship.

6. It is written by another unknown James.

7. It is written by someone who uses the name James to increase the authority of his letter. This practice of pseudonymous authorship, that is, of writing in the name of a famous teacher, was known in the ancient world. The central argument for this position is that the Greek of the letter of James is too elegant to have been written by a Palestinian peasant such as the brother of Jesus. It must, therefore, have been written by a more literate writer who used his name. However, recent scholarship has shown that Palestine was quite cosmopolitan in the first century. So, it is impossible to say how fluent a Palestinian Jew might be in Greek.

Others claim that James 2:14-26 is reacting to the teaching of Paul's epistles on faith and works. Thus, it must be written after Paul's letters and so after the lifetime of James the Lord's brother. If this is the case, some argue, then the letter is pseudonymous. However, it is not clear that James reacts to Paul (see the commentary on James 2:14-26 below). Even if he is, he could be responding to Paul before Romans and Galatians are penned.

It is likely then that the letter was written by a well-known James. The son of Zebedee and the brother of Jesus were the two most famous persons with this name in the early church. James the son of Zebedee was martyred too early to have written this letter. Therefore, James, the brother of Jesus and Jude, is most likely the author. This has been the traditional consensus of the church through the ages.

The content of the letter is consistent with the view that James the brother of the Lord is its author. The writer is well-known and speaks authoritatively. He knows the teachings of Jesus. He knows the climate, vegetation, and social setting of Palestine. Specifically he mentions the scorching wind (1:11), good and bad water (3:11), figs, olives and grapes (3:12) and the need for early and late rain (5:7). Such knowledge does not prove that the book was written by someone from Palestine but does make it plausible.

THE BROTHERS OF JESUS

The brothers of Jesus, including James and Jude, were prominent leaders in the early church. There is some disagreement over the meaning of "brothers." Some scholars, particularly Roman Catholics who believe in the perpetual virginity of Mary, think the word refers to cousins or other relatives of Jesus. However, the Greek word rarely permits this meaning but is used just as our English word "brother." It is possible that these are Joseph's sons by a previous marriage but more likely that these are the younger children of Joseph and Mary.

These brothers are named in Matthew 13:55 (also Mark 6:3): "Isn't this the carpenter's son? Isn't his mother's name Mary, and aren't his brothers James, Joseph, Simon, and Judas? Aren't all his sisters with us?" Since Matthew and Mark were written several years later than the events they portray, it is likely they mention the brothers of Jesus by name because they were well-known in the early church. James is the first name on this list in both Matthew and Mark, so we assume he is the oldest brother next to Jesus. Judas (or Jude) is last in Matthew but next to last in Mark; thus, he is one of the youngest brothers.

John plainly says the brothers of Jesus did not believe in him during his ministry (John 7:5). On one occasion they actively opposed him: "When his family heard about this, they went to take charge of him, for they said, 'He is out of his mind'" (Mark 3:21). Thinking Jesus was crazy, they sought to have him committed. No wonder Jesus later disclaims his mother and brothers when they come to see him. "'Who are my mother and my brothers?' he asked. Then he looked at those seated in a circle around him and said, 'Here are my mother and my brothers! Whoever does God's will is my brother and sister and mother" (Mark 3:32b-35). His brothers' lack of faith may explain why Jesus on the cross committed his mother to John's care, not to theirs (John 19:26-27). The memory of their unbelief may also be behind the refusal of James and Jude to call themselves brothers of Jesus in their letters, preferring the title "slave of Jesus Christ" (James 1:1; Jude 1).

However after the resurrection and ascension of Jesus, his brothers were with the apostles and others at prayer in the upper room (Acts 1:14). What changed them into believers? They had seen the risen Lord. Paul tells us Jesus appeared to James after the resurrection (1 Corinthians 15:7), and although we are not specifically told, it seems likely he appeared to his other brothers, perhaps as part of the five hundred who saw him at the same time (1 Corinthians 15:6).

James was the best known of the brothers and a leader of the Jerusalem church. When Peter is miraculously released from prison, he wants it reported to "James and the brothers" (Acts 12:17). The judgment given by James wins the day at the Jerusalem council of Acts 15. As leader of the Jewish believers in Jerusalem, James persuades Paul to perform a purification rite in the temple to prove his loyalty to the law (Acts 21:17-26).

The unity between Paul and James in Acts is less evident in Galatians, where Paul calls James one of those in Jerusalem "who seemed to be important" and "reputed to be pillars" (Galatians 2:6,9), perhaps implying that James was not as important as he thought himself to be. Later, men come from James and lead Peter and Barnabas into hypocrisy over refusing to eat with Gentiles (Galatians 2:12). However, the differences between James and Paul should not be overstated. James is concerned that Jewish believers continue to obey the Law as they should. Paul does not want the Law to be forced on Gentiles. In both Acts and Galatians, James and Paul agree that God has called one to minister to the Jews, the other to the Gentiles (Acts 15; Galatians 2:9).

Although James was the best known, the other brothers of Jesus were also Christian leaders. Paul claims the right to take a believing wife along on his journeys as do "the Lord's brothers" (1 Corinthians 9:5). Thus, the brothers of Jesus, including James and Jude, were traveling missionaries in the early church, and so were known and respected by many. Because of their childhood memories of growing up with Jesus and their later experiences of serving the risen Lord, James and Jude are uniquely qualified to speak to Christians in the letters that bear their names.

DATE AND OCCASION

The question of the date of James is connected with the discussion of its authorship. Some who think it is pseudonymous would date it quite late in the first century. However, if it is by James the brother of the Lord, then it must date somewhere between the time he became a leader of the Jerusalem church (about A.D. 40) and his death (about A.D. 62). If it is before the Jerusalem meeting of A.D. 50 (Acts 15), then the dispersion he refers to in v.1 might be the scattering of the church during the persecution by Saul (Acts 8:1). If it is dated that early, it is chronologically the first book of the New Testament. However, James refers often to quotations from the Sermon on the Mount in his letter.[1] He most likely is quoting from an oral tradition of the Sermon but possibly is familiar with Matthew's account. If he indeed knew Matthew's Gospel, then James wrote his letter toward the end of his life.

There are few hints in James of its setting or destination. James the Lord's brother was a leader of the church in Jerusalem. Many scholars thus find a Palestinian setting for the letter. As shown above, the content of the letter is consistent with a Palestinian setting. It is addressed to "the twelve tribes scattered among the nations" (v. 1). This broad address makes it impossible to define the situation of the recipients of the letter. James is truly a general or catholic (that is, universal) epistle. Since we do not know the specific circumstances of the original readers, this commentary will not speculate on that subject but will focus on the universal application of James' teaching for the church throughout the ages.

STRUCTURE, THEMES, AND STYLE

James is a letter in form; it has a greeting, refers to its readers often as "brothers," and identifies its author by name. However, it is a letter in form only; there are no greetings to persons by name and no mention of the circumstances of author or readers.

James is thus a letter in form, but in essence it is another type of literature, paraenesis or ethical instruction. The Greek philosophers gave such moral instruction in the ancient world. Proverbs is an Old Testament book of morals. Even

---

[1]Peter H. Davids, "James and Jesus," in David Wenham, ed. *Gospel Perspectives*, vol. 5 (Sheffield: JSOT Press, 1985), pp. 63-84. See below in the introduction and the commentary for discussion of specific passages where James quotes or refers to the Sermon on the Mount.

earlier, Leviticus gives moral instruction to Israel, especially in the "Holiness Code" of Leviticus 19. James often refers to that chapter in his book:[2]

James	Quotation from Leviticus
2:1	19:15
2:8	19:18
2:9	19:15
4:11	19:16
5:4	19:13
5:9	19:18
5:12	19:12
5:20	19:17

James was also influenced by certain Apocryphal books that taught similar moral maxims. The Apocrypha refers to those books found in certain Greek and Latin translations of the Old Testament that are not accepted as Scripture by Jews or by Protestants. As is seen in the following chart, two of those books, Ecclesiasticus (also known as Sirach, written c. 180 B.C.) and the Wisdom of Solomon (written c. 30 B.C.), have passages that are strikingly similar to certain verses in James:

Topic	James	Ecclesiasticus	Wisdom
Patience	1:2-4	1:23	
Wisdom	1:5	1:26	
Doubt	1:6-8	1:28	
Trials	1:12	2:1-5	
Temptation	1:13	15:11-12	
Hearing	1:19	5:11	
Rich and Poor	2:6	13:19	2:10
Mercy	2:13		6:6
Brevity of life	4:13-16		5:8-14

---

[2]See Luke Timothy Johnson, "The Use of Leviticus 19 in the Letter of James," *Journal of Biblical Literature* 101 (1982), 391-401.

Topic	James	Ecclesiasticus	Wisdom
Money Rusts	5:3	29:10	
Righteous Killed	5:6		2:12, 20
Pray for Sick	5:14	38:9	

Comparing these passages, it is obvious that James knew and used these books. However, he does not quote them as inspired Scripture. He is following in the same tradition of passing on moral wisdom. Thus, like these and other books of moral teaching, James is loosely organized, tying together related ethical teachings by use of repeated terms. It is difficult to find an overarching theme to the book or divide it into major sections. Instead, James continues to come back to a few important subjects. Although this commentary will proceed verse-by-verse through James, another profitable way of studying the book is to look at it topically. James addresses six major themes in the book:

1. Waiting for the Lord (James 1:2-4, 12-18; 5:7-12).
2. Wisdom (James 1:5-8; 3:13-18).
3. Rich and Poor (James 1:9-11; 2:1-13; 4:13-16; 5:1-6).
4. The Tongue (James 1:19-21,26; 3:1-12; 4:11-12).
5. Prayer (James 1:6-8; 4:1-10; 5:13-20).
6. Faith and Action (James 1:22-27; 2:14-26).

James has a vigorous and fresh writing style. He generally uses short and vivid sentences. He is fond of making comparisons to nature—waves, sun, flowers, planets, animals—to give his teaching concrete expression. He asks his readers short, penetrating questions to cause them to reflect. Sometimes he uses the form of the diatribe, a scathing denunciation of immoral behavior. All these literary uses are common in moral literature.

JAMES AND THE SERMON ON THE MOUNT

There are so many parallels between James and the teaching of Jesus in Matthew 5-7 and Luke 6 and 11 that James can best be thought of as a commentary on the Sermon on the Mount. There are more parallels between James and Matthew, but the language of the allusions is more similar to Luke.[3] This could mean that James knew the Gospels of Matthew and Luke. However, it is more likely that James knew the sermon through oral tradition, since the early church would be sure to preserve the ethical teaching of Jesus. The following chart shows that every section of James has an echo of the Sermon:

Topic in James	Sermon on the Mount
Trials (1:2-4)	Matthew 5:10-12, 48; Luke 6:23
Asking (1:5-8)	Matthew 7:7-8; Luke 11:9-10
Riches (1:9-11)	Matthew 6:19-21
God's Gifts (1:12-18)	Matthew 7:11; Luke 11:13
Listening (1:19-27)	Matthew 5:22; 7:21-27; Luke 6:46-49
Judging (2:1-13)	Matthew 5:3,5,7,19-22; 7:1-5; Luke 6:20
Faith and Works (2:14-26)	Matthew 7:21-23
The Tongue (3:1-12)	Matthew 7:16; Luke 6:44-45
Wisdom (3:13-18)	Matthew 5:5-9
The World or God (4:1-10)	Matthew 5:4, 8; 6:7-8, 24; 7:7-8; Luke 6:25
Slander (4:11-12)	Matthew 5:21-22; 7:1; Luke 6:37
Tomorrow (4:13-17)	Matthew 6:25-34
The Rich (5:1-6)	Matthew 6:19-21; Luke 6:24-25; 12:33
Patience (5:7-11)	Matthew 5:11-12; 7:1; Luke 6:22-23

---

[3]For more on the parallels between James and the Sermon on the Mount, see Patrick J. Hartin, *James and the Q Sayings of Jesus* (Sheffield: JSOT Press, 1991), pp. 140-172.

Topic in James	Sermon on the Mount
Swearing (5:12)	Matthew 5:33-37
Prayer (5:13-18)	Matthew 6:12-15; 7:7-11

These parallels are discussed in the commentary. Some are near verbatim quotations from the Sermon on the Mount; some are clear references; some are only vague allusions. However, the recognition that James is intentionally relating the teachings of Jesus to the situation of his readers increases one's appreciation for the book. As we will see below, James is no legalist but one who serves the church by calling it back to what Jesus intended it to be, a community that practices a higher righteousness (Matthew 5:20).

THE VALUE OF JAMES

There are two widespread misunderstandings of James that must be avoided to appreciate its value. One is that James is a legalistic book. Martin Luther (1483-1546) called it "an epistle of straw," meaning it had little value because he could not find the gospel there. Luther and many after him misunderstood the teaching of James on faith and works. As we will show below in the commentary, James did not believe in works righteousness but, like Paul, taught that Christians are saved by an active faith.

A more recent version of "James the legalist" is held by scholars who say James only repeats Jewish moral instruction, so there is nothing specifically Christian in his teaching. It is true that much of James is Jewish moral teaching. So is most of the moral teaching of Jesus. Since Jesus came to fulfill the Law and Prophets (Matthew 5:17), how can it be otherwise? James repeats the moral teaching from the Sermon on the Mount. However, James (like Jesus) takes conventional moral wisdom (both Jewish and Greek) and redefines it in light of the incarnation and the sure return of Christ. James's ethic is thus eschatological (from the Greek word ἔσχατος, *eschatos,* "last," that is the last days). He tells Christians how to live as they wait for Christ's return. Thus, James is a thoroughly Christian book.

The second misunderstanding is that James is a practical book; it deals with people where they are and gives concrete steps on how they can improve. Of course, James is practical if one means he is concerned with Christian living. His words are certainly relevant to contemporary Christians. To show that relevance, every section of the commentary will end with a summary and application of James's teaching to Christian living today.

However, by calling James "practical" some mean it simply enforces our own cultural values. Such could not be farther from the truth. James is a thoroughly impractical book in that he challenges our assumptions at every turn. He condemns human wisdom and is pessimistic of the ability of humans to reform themselves. He is hopeful, however, of God's transcendent power in the believer. By calling on his readers to receive "wisdom from above" (James 3:17), he fights worldliness in the church by calling Christians to wait patiently for the Lord's return. If we feel comfortable with the teaching of James (or rather, with the teaching of Jesus, since he is the original source of James's teaching), then we have probably misunderstood it. It is a radical, counter-cultural message that the church today needs to hear and do.

OUTLINE

    I. GREETING — 1:1
   II. ENDURING TRIALS — 1:2-4
  III. ASK FOR WISDOM — 1:5-8
  IV. RICHES TEMPORARY — 1:9-11
   V. TEMPTATION NOT FROM GOD — 1:12-18
  VI. SPEAKING, LISTENING, DOING — 1:19-27
 VII. JUDGING BY APPEARANCE — 2:1-13

      A. Favoritism — 2:1–7

      B. The Royal Law — 2:8–13

VIII. FAITH THAT WORKS — 2:14-26

      A. Faith Without Works — 2:14–17

      B. Faith With Works — 2:18–26

  IX. TAMING THE TONGUE — 3:1-12
   X. WISDOM, EARTHLY AND HEAVENLY — 3:13-18
  XI. FRIENDS OF THE WORLD OR OF GOD — 4:1-10
 XII. DON'T SPEAK AGAINST A BROTHER — 4:11-12
XIII. DON'T COUNT ON TOMORROW — 4:13-17
XIV. WARNING TO THE RICH — 5:1-6
 XV. WAITING FOR THE LORD — 5:7-11
XVI. DON'T SWEAR — 5:12
XVII. PRAYER, CONFESSION, AND SAVING THE SINNER — 5:13-20

BIBLIOGRAPHY
JAMES

Adamson, James. *The Epistle of James.* New International Commentary. Grand Rapids: Eerdmans, 1976.

———. *James: The Man and His Message.* Grand Rapids: Eerdmans, 1989.

Davids, Peter H. *The Epistle of James.* New International Greek Testament. Grand Rapids: Eerdmans, 1982.

Dibelius, Martin. *James.* Hermeneia. Philadelphia: Fortress, 1976.

Hort, F.J.A. *The Epistle of St. James.* London: Macmillan, 1909.

Johnson, Luke Timothy. *The Letter of James.* Anchor Bible. New York: Doubleday, 1995.

Kistemaker, Simon J. *James and I-III John.* New Testament Commentary. Grand Rapids: Baker, 1986.

Knowling, R.J. *The Epistle of St. James.* Westminster Commentaries. London: Methuen and Co., 1904.

Kugelman, Richard. *James & Jude.* New Testament Message. Wilmington, DE: Michael Glazier, 1980.

Laws, Sophie. *A Commentary on the Epistle of James.* Harper New Testament Commentary. New York: Harper, 1980.

Martin, R.A. *James.* Augsburg Commentary on the New Testament. Minneapolis: Augsburg, 1982.

Martin, Ralph P. *James.* Word Biblical Commentary. Waco: Word, 1988.

Mayor, Joseph B. *The Epistle of St. James.* London: Macmillan, 1897.

McDonnell, Rea. *The Catholic Epistles and Hebrews.* Wilmington, DE: Michael Glazier, 1986.

Mitton, C. Leslie. *The Epistle of James.* Grand Rapids: Eerdmans, 1966.

Moo, Douglas J. *James.* Tyndale New Testament Commentary. Grand Rapids: Eerdmans, 1985.

Motyer, Alec. *The Message of James.* The Bible Speaks Today. Downers Grove: IVP, 1988.

Perkins, Pheme. *1,2 Peter, James, Jude.* Interpretation. Louisville: John Knox, 1995.

Plummer, Alfred. *The General Epistles of St. James and St. Jude.* London: Hodder and Stoughton, 1891.

Reicke, Bo. *The Epistles of James, Peter, and Jude.* Anchor Bible. New York: Doubleday, 1964.

Roberts, J.W. *The Letter of James.* Living Word Commentary. Abilene: ACU Press, 1963.

Ropes, James Hardy. *James.* International Critical Commentary. Edinburgh: T&T Clark, 1916.

Ross, Alexander. *The Epistles of James and Jude.* New International Commentary. Grand Rapids: Eerdmans, 1954.

Sidebottom, E.M. *James, Jude, 2 Peter.* New Century Bible. Grand Rapids: Eerdmans, 1967.

Stulac, George M. *James.* IVP New Testament Commentary. Downers Grove: IVP, 1993.

Tasker, R.V.G. *The General Epistle of James.* Tyndale New Testament Commentary. Grand Rapids: Eerdmans, 1957.

JAMES 1

I. GREETING (1:1)

**¹James, a servant of God and of the Lord Jesus Christ,
To the twelve tribes scattered among the nations:
Greetings.**

James opens his letter in the usual way by identifying the author and the readers and by giving a word of greeting. His opening, however, is quite brief. He does not identify himself as the brother of Christ but simply as the servant (δοῦλος, *doulos*, "slave") of God and Christ. This use of "slave" to describe one's relationship to God is found in pagan literature, in the Old Testament (Joshua 14:7; 24:29; 2 Samuel 7:8; Psalm 135:1; Isaiah 42:19; Amos 3:7), and in the New Testament (Acts 2:18; 4:29; Romans 1:1; Philippians 1:1; 2 Peter 1:1). Even Jesus himself took on the form of a slave (Philippians 2:7). The widespread use of the term should not blind one to its significance. To be a slave of God and Christ is to do their bidding without fail. No greater title can be sought by the Christian than slave. James writes to teach his readers how to be good slaves of the Lord Jesus.

James addresses "the twelve tribes scattered among the nations" (literally "in the Diaspora"). The Diaspora was the name for Jews living outside Palestine, perhaps implying he writes from within Palestine. Does James write to all Jews outside Palestine? No, for the content of James is clearly Christian. He therefore writes to Jewish Christians, to those Jews who have accepted Jesus as the Christ or Messiah (cf. 1 Peter 1:1; Revelation 7:4-9). His greeting may even include

Gentile Christians who also believe in Jesus as Messiah. Those believers are the true Israel, the twelve tribes God has promised to save (Romans 9:24-26; 1 Peter 2:9-10; Revelation 7:3-8).

If the letter of James is dated quite early, then Diaspora could refer to those who "were scattered throughout Judea and Samaria" (Acts 8:1) as a result of persecution from Saul. If so, James is writing to Jewish Christians who had been part of the church he led in Jerusalem.

By calling his readers "the Diaspora" or those "scattered among the nations," James may also be giving a hint to one of the major thrusts of his letter. Those who accept Jesus as the Messiah are scattered among the nations and belong only to redeemed Israel, the twelve tribes. They are in the world but do not belong to it (John 15:18-19). They live as aliens and exiles who look for a better home (1 Peter 1:17; 2:11; Hebrews 11:8-16; 13:14). James writes to show what it means morally to live as a scattered people who owe allegiance to Christ, not to the standards of the world.

"Greetings" is the typical address of a Greek letter. However, such a brief greeting is unusual in the New Testament. It is found only here, in the greeting of the Roman commander Claudius Lysias to Governor Felix (Acts 23:26), and in the letter of the apostles and elders in Jerusalem to Gentile Christians (Acts 15:23). If the letter from Jerusalem in Acts 15 was composed by James, the Lord's brother, then this would be his usual way of greeting fellow Christians in letters.

Section Summary and Application:

Just as James calls himself the slave of God and Christ, so Christians today should remember that the greatest in the kingdom is the one who serves (Mark 10:42-45). We also, like James's original readers, are scattered throughout the nations. We live in whatever country God has placed us in, but our ultimate citizenship is in heaven. James reminds us not to be too comfortable in the world.

II. ENDURING TRIALS (1:2-4)

²Consider it pure joy, my brothers, whenever you face trials of many kinds, ³because you know that the testing of your faith develops perseverance. ⁴Perseverance must finish its work so that you may be mature and complete, not lacking anything.

1:2 Consider it pure joy, my brothers,

Fourteen times in this letter, James addresses his readers as "brothers." This language is found throughout the New Testament, implying both the closeness and the responsibility of being family. James's frequent use of "brother" gives his letter a pastoral tone; he is writing to encourage them in the faith as a brother who is a fellow servant of Christ. "Brothers," of course, includes sisters as well; James specifically mentions sisters as readers in 2:15. Throughout this commentary we will also use James's language of "brothers" to include sisters in Christ.

Stress and pressure are not purely modern experiences. The readers of James also faced trials. The brothers are to consider these trials to be pure (in Greek, πᾶσαν, *pasan*, "all") joy. All or pure joy indicates sincerity. Christians are not merely to put the best face on trouble and try to look on the bright side but should sincerely rejoice when trouble comes. The joy the brothers have in trials is not pleasure (they do not enjoy pain) but rather "eschatological anticipated joy."[1] In other words, the brothers rejoice not because they suffer now, but because they know suffering is preparing them for the anticipated return of Christ.

whenever you face trials of many kinds,

"Trials" (πειρασμός, *peirasmos*) is an ambiguous word that may refer to the ordinary troubles of life, to persecution for the faith, or to temptation to do evil (see 1:12-13). "Many

---

[1] Peter Davids, *The Epistle of James*. The New International Greek Commentary (Grand Rapids: Eerdmans, 1982), p. 66.

kinds" (literally "multicolored") implies James includes all these meanings in verses 2-4. Christians should not intentionally choose suffering. Literally in Greek, James says the brothers fall into trials. They do not seek them, but they come. To be human is to suffer. These trials are not chosen but fall upon the believers unexpectedly. The New Testament does not clearly answer the questions of the origin of evil or why bad things happen to good people. James does show that God is so great that he can use what is evil for his children's ultimate good. Believers do not want trials to come. Jesus taught his disciples to pray for deliverance from evil (Matthew 6:13), but when faced with trials of all kinds and colors, the Christian should consider them pure joy.

1:3 because you know that the testing of your faith develops perseverance.

This joy comes because the Christian knows that trials are also tests of faith (cf. 1 Peter 1:7). One is reminded of those Old Testament heroes like Abraham (Genesis 22:1-18) and Job who passed the tests of faith. They are tests of faith because they teach the brothers to trust in God alone. Passing these tests leads to perseverance (ὑπομονή, *hypomone,* cf. Romans 5:3). This is a rich word in Greek implying steadfastness, fortitude, constancy, persistent determination, strong consistency, and staying power. The best translation might be "heroic endurance." Standing the trials of life produces more than a passive patience or a cynical resignation; it gives (in the words of the hymn by William H. Bathurst) "a faith that will not shrink, tho' pressed by every foe."

1:4 Perseverance must finish its work so that you may be mature and complete, not lacking anything.

But even this heroic endurance is not an end within itself. It must be allowed to finish its work, to grow into "perfection" (τέλειος, *teleios,* a word James uses more often than any other New Testament writer). Perfection in the New Testament does not mean without flaw or error but indicates (as translated here in the NIV) maturity and completeness. The perfect person has reached his intended end.

Enduring trials thus produces joy because such tests shape believers into the image of Christ. In that image one lacks nothing. Perfection in James is not just the result of our own efforts; it does not come from a "works righteousness." Instead, it is brought by God and is the end of steadfast obedience. Here James echoes Jesus at the Sermon on the Mount, who urged his hearers, "Be perfect, therefore, as your heavenly Father is perfect" (Matthew 5:48).

Section Summary and Application:

In his opening lines, James challenges the standards of the world. Worldly wisdom can see no value in suffering. It says pain is to be avoided at all costs, and only pleasure brings happiness. By contrast, to Christians even trials are a joy because they lead us to maturity in Christ. Christians judge value quite differently than the world does. To us the highest value is not freedom from pain but a faith that perseveres. The suffering that life brings, although bad in itself, can be turned by God into pure joy.

III. ASK FOR WISDOM (1:5-8)

⁵If any of you lacks wisdom, he should ask God, who gives generously to all without finding fault, and it will be given to him. ⁶But when he asks, he must believe and not doubt, because he who doubts is like a wave of the sea, blown and tossed by the wind. ⁷That man should not think he will receive anything from the Lord; ⁸he is a double-minded man, unstable in all he does.

1:5 If any of you lacks wisdom,

The heroic endurance that comes from facing trials is to make one complete, "not lacking anything." Yet all believers lack one thing: wisdom. No matter how much wisdom they have, the brothers can always use more. It particularly requires wisdom to see trials as a blessing. James encourages them to ask God for it.

Wisdom is an important biblical word. It means more than intellectual knowledge. Wisdom is less "knowing that" than "knowing how." It implies a skill in living that is passed down from parent to child and has its ultimate source in God. One is reminded of the Wisdom books in the Old Testament — Proverbs, Ecclesiastes, and Job — that say, "The fear of the Lord is the beginning of wisdom" (Proverbs 1:7). On the one hand, Proverbs urges one to be always "turning your ear to wisdom and applying your heart to understanding" (Proverbs 2:2); on the other, it reminds, "For the Lord gives wisdom, and from his mouth come knowledge and understanding" (Proverbs 2:6).

he should ask God,

Asking for wisdom reminds one of the most famous wise man of all, Solomon. God appeared to him in a dream and offered to give him anything he asked. Solomon asked for wisdom, not riches and honor. God is so pleased with this choice, that he grants Solomon all three gifts. James agrees that wisdom is not from our own efforts but is a gift from God (cf. 1 Corinthians 1:26-2:16; Philippians 3:15).

who gives generously to all without finding fault, and it will be given to him.

God gives wisdom generously (ἁπλῶς, *haplos*, a word found only here in the New Testament). The word means he gives "straightforwardly," that is, with no strings attached. Unlike the "double-minded man" (v.8), God is not in doubt about his giving. God has no ulterior motives. He gives without hesitation and without regard to our worthiness. He gives "to all." Unlike humans (James 2:1-4), God has no favorites. He also gives "without finding fault." God is no reluctant, critical giver but a generous Father (cf. Matthew 7:7-11). He is eager to give wisdom to those who ask.

1:6 But when he asks, he must believe and not doubt,

As God has no doubt about his giving, one must ask in faith, not doubt. Since God is a generous Father, Christians must be willing to receive as children. Faith is connected with the granting of prayer requests in many New Testament passages (Matthew 8:10; 9:28; Mark 2:5; 4:40; 5:34-36; 9:23-24; 11:23-24; Romans 4:20-21). Faith here is not a general term for Christian belief but refers to the certainty that the request will be fulfilled. Although Christians are always to pray that God's will be done, they can be confident that it is always God's will to give them more wisdom.

because he who doubts is like a wave of the sea, blown and tossed by the wind.

To doubt that God will hear their requests for wisdom is to doubt his generosity and character. Such a doubter is like a wave blown by the wind, a common metaphor in ancient literature for indecision.

1:7 That man should not think he will receive anything from the Lord; 1:8 he is a double-minded man, unstable in all he does.

He is double-minded (δίψυχος, *dipsychos*, literally "double-souled"), an interesting word found only in James in the New Testament.[2] He has enough faith to ask for wisdom but not enough to be confident he will receive. He puts his hand to the plow and then looks back (Luke 9:62). Ironically, it is this very doubt that keeps him from receiving. Such an indecisive and fickle person cannot be trusted to be consistent in anything he does. His instability is in stark contrast to the perseverance or strong consistency produced by enduring trial (v. 4).

Section Summary and Application:

Wisdom is one gift needed by Christians throughout the ages. It is particularly needed in our time, when the forces of

---

[2]Stanley E. Porter, "Is *dipsychos* (James 1,8; 4,8) a 'Christian' Word?", *Biblica* 71 (1990), 469-498.

secularization and worldliness threaten the church. We need wisdom to view the trials of this age as pure joy. Such wisdom does not come naturally from our own abilities and efforts. It is God's gift alone. We should pray regularly for this wisdom, trusting that God will freely give it to guide his people. All our prayers should go to God with confidence, not doubt.

IV. RICHES TEMPORARY (1:9-11)

⁹The brother in humble circumstances ought to take pride in his high position. ¹⁰But the one who is rich should take pride in his low position, because he will pass away like a wild flower. ¹¹For the sun rises with scorching heat and withers the plant; its blossom falls and its beauty is destroyed. In the same way, the rich man will fade away even while he goes about his business.

1:9 The brother in humble circumstances

In these verses, James introduces a theme he will return to often in his letter: the relation of rich and poor. He speaks of "the brother in humble circumstances." The word here means "humble" or "lowly" in most contexts; in this one it refers primarily to the economically lowly, the poor in contrast to the rich (v.10).

ought to take pride in his high position.

A poor Christian ("brother") should boast or take pride in his high position. Boasting is condemned elsewhere in the New Testament and in James (Romans 2:17,23; 3:27; 1 Corinthians 1:29; 4:7; 5:6; 2 Corinthians 5:12; 11:18; Galatians 6:13; Ephesians 2:9; James 4:16). However, rejoicing in what God has done in Christ, "boasting in the Lord," is approved (Romans 5:2-3, 11; 1 Corinthians 1:31; 2 Corinthians 10:13-17; Philippians 3:3). Here the poor are urged to boast not in their own ability, but in what God has done for them. Although they are humble and poor from an earthly standpoint, God has "chosen those who are poor in the eyes of the world to be rich in faith and to inherit the kingdom he promised to those who love him" (James 2:5). True wealth is measured not in money but in faith.

1:10 But the one who is rich should take pride in his low position,

By contrast, the rich are brought low. James does not call the rich person "brother" as he does the humble. He is likely contrasting not rich and poor in the church, but the rich of the world with the lowly Christians. The concept of boasting or taking pride in being humbled is interesting. By contemplating the temporary nature of wealth, the rich may learn humility before God and turn to him for salvation. Yet this humiliation is not just an inner attitude but a reversal in status; the poor are exalted and the rich brought low (Matthew 23:12; Luke 14:11; 18:14).

because he will pass away like a wild flower.

The great reversal of rich and poor is a theme found throughout both Testaments and is particularly important in the Gospel of Luke.[3] One thinks of the switch in positions between the rich man and Lazarus (Luke 16:25). God will turn the shame of the poor into pride and will humble the boastful rich. Again, one hears echoes of the Beatitudes in the Sermon on the Mount: "Blessed are you who are poor" (Luke 6:20), and "Blessed are the meek, for they will inherit the earth" (Matthew 5:5). Christians should not pursue wealth because it is transitory and because they are already rich toward God. It is that spiritual wealth that makes them boast.

1:11 For the sun rises with scorching heat and withers the plant; its blossom falls and its beauty is destroyed.

The brief nature of earthly wealth is illustrated by the well-

---

[3]See John O. York, *The Last Shall Be First: The Rhetoric of Reversal in Luke* (Sheffield: JSOT Press, 1991).

known Jewish image of plants scorched by the heat. In the climate of Palestine, the hot sun and wind can kill fragile flowers in less than a day (cf. Ezekiel 17:10). No wonder this was a favorite image of Old Testament writers for the transitory nature not just of riches but of life itself (Psalm 103:15-16; Isaiah 40:6-8). The beauty of the flower is destroyed just as the outward beauty of the rich — gold rings and fine clothes (James 2:2) — fades away. One remembers Jesus' words about riches being stolen or destroyed while heavenly treasure lasts (Matthew 6:19-21). Money promises security and permanence but cannot deliver them.

In the same way, the rich man will fade away even while he goes about his business.

The rich will fade, literally "in the middle of his travels." James has in mind not just those born to wealth but those traveling merchants who pursue it. Those who obtain wealth through their own hard work are particularly prone to pride: "I work hard for my money; I deserve to enjoy it." James thinks this attitude foolish. The mad dash for success only causes one to fade away as in the parable of the rich man whose life is required of him the very night of his greatest financial triumph (Luke 12:13-21).

Section Summary and Application:

Jesus was always hard on the rich (cf. Matthew 19:16-26; Mark 12:41-44; Luke 6:24; 12:16-21; 14:12; 16:19-31; 18:25). As will be seen, James also always portrays the poor as righteous (cf. Amos 2:6; 5:12) and the rich as evil (Isaiah 53:9). As with all generalizations, there will certainly be exceptions. There are wealthy persons who are faithful Christians, and there are poor people who reject Christ. However, we should resist the temptation to spiritualize these passages by making "poor" merely a term for the community of the faithful. James's warning is clear; riches are to be viewed not as a sign of grace or a benign blessing but at best as a snare and a temptation and at worst a sign of judgment.

It is particularly difficult for the average American to realize that compared to most of the world we are rich, and so the warning of James is to us. We will be exalted if we are rich, but only if we understand the low value of our wealth and the true value of faith. Only by humble reception of the gift of God can the impossible happen; even the rich can be saved (Matthew 19:26).

V. TEMPTATION NOT FROM GOD (1:12-18)

¹²**Blessed is the man who perseveres under trial, because when he has stood the test, he will receive the crown of life that God has promised to those who love him.**

¹³**When tempted, no one should say, "God is tempting me." For God cannot be tempted by evil, nor does he tempt anyone;** ¹⁴**but each one is tempted when, by his own evil desire, he is dragged away and enticed.** ¹⁵**Then, after desire has conceived, it gives birth to sin; and sin, when it is full-grown, gives birth to death.**

¹⁶**Don't be deceived, my dear brothers.** ¹⁷**Every good and perfect gift is from above, coming down from the Father of the heavenly lights, who does not change like shifting shadows.** ¹⁸**He chose to give us birth through the word of truth, that we might be a kind of firstfruits of all he created.**

1:12 Blessed is the man who perseveres under trial,

James returns to the topic of enduring trials (see vv. 2-4). The word for trial (πειρασμός, *peirasmos*) is the same here as above in verses 2-4 and below in verses 13-14. Here in verse 12, it implies persecution and trouble, not temptation, for temptation should be resisted, not just endured.

The one who endures trials is blessed, a word used frequently in Psalms and Proverbs (e.g., "Blessed is the man . . . ," Psalm 1:1) and in the Beatitudes of the Sermon on the Mount (Matthew 5:1-12). "Blessed" (μακάριος, *makarios*) is a deeper word than "happy," implying that deep and lasting joy that comes only as a gift from God.

because when he has stood the test, he will receive the crown of life that God has promised to those who love him.

The one who endures the test will be blessed by God with the crown of life, probably not a royal crown but the garland of flowers given to victors in ancient athletic contests. Unlike the rich who fade like a flower (v. 10), those who endure trials and finish the race will receive the garland of life that never fades (cf. 1 Corinthians 9:25; 2 Timothy 4:8; 1 Peter 5:4; Revelation 2:10). God (or perhaps Jesus, the Greek merely says, "he") promises this crown to those who love him. All Christians, not just a particularly favored few, are called to be heroes, to stand the test and receive the crown of life.

1:13 When tempted, no one should say, "God is tempting me."

James then turns to another type of trial, temptation. Although the word in Greek is the same here as in verse 12, the context clearly implies temptation, not just any test. James counters the charge that it is God who tempts. Why would anyone make such a charge? Perhaps it stems from a misunderstanding of the sovereignty of God; if this is truly God's world, then evil as well as good must come from him. Perhaps blaming God is just the human way to escape blame: "A man's folly ruins his life, yet his heart rages against the Lord" (Proverbs 19:3). Adam blamed, "the woman you put here with me" (Genesis 3:12) for the first sin and so indirectly blamed God. Human beings have tried to shift blame from themselves ever since.

The specific occasion for this charge against God might be a misunderstanding of the teaching of Jesus in the Sermon on the Mount. From other passages in James, it is clear that he and his readers knew the sermon. They, therefore, remembered that Jesus taught his disciples to pray, "And lead us not into temptation, but deliver us from the evil one" (Matthew

6:13; cf. Matthew 26:41; Mark 14:38; Luke 22:46). If tempted, one might erroneously conclude that God had led one there or at least he had failed to protect from temptation.

For God cannot be tempted by evil, nor does he tempt anyone;

James battles this misunderstanding by stating emphatically that God does not tempt. Before that statement, he has another that is hard to interpret: God is "untemptable" (ἀπείραστος, *apeirastos*, a word used only here in the New Testament). Some have suggested this means, "God's goodness ought not to be questioned or tested."[4] Thus, to blame God for sin is to test him, yet he does not test or tempt. More likely, the word should be translated as in the NIV: "God cannot be tempted." Although it is not immediately clear how this leads to the conclusion that he does not tempt, there is a connection. God has no acquaintance with evil at all. It cannot touch him. Therefore, he cannot lead others to do evil.

God tests his people, but he does not tempt them. In the Old Testament, God tested Abraham (Genesis 22:1), the people of Israel (Judges 2:22), and Hezekiah (2 Chronicles 32:31). God's testing of Israel in the wilderness was actually a sign of his love. He showed they were his children by disciplining them as a father does his son (Deuteronomy 8:2-5). The difference between God's testing and temptation is that he wants his people to pass the test and to win the crown. He even provides a way of escape from temptation (1 Corinthians 10:13). When the evil one tempts, he wants them to fail. Therefore, temptation never comes from God.

1:14 but each one is tempted when, by his own evil desire, he is dragged away and enticed.

Where does temptation come from? James might have said, "From Satan, the evil one," but he does not. Instead he places the responsibility for temptation on the individual: "his

---

[4]Peter H. Davids, "The Meaning of *Apeirastos* in James 1:13," *New Testament Studies* 24 (1978), 386-392.

own (the Greek word ἴδιος, *idios*, is emphatic here) desire leads him astray." Desire can be either positive or negative in the New Testament, depending on the context. Here it is evil desire that drags away and entices. The Greek words (ἐξέλκω, *exelkō*, and δελεάζω, *deleazō*) here are fishing terms. Desire baits us and reels us in.

1:15 Then, after desire has conceived, it gives birth to sin; and sin, when it is full-grown, gives birth to death.

This evil desire (ἐπιθυμία, *epithymia*), if left unchecked, has severe consequences. The process is compared to human growth. Desire conceives, gives birth to sin, which matures into death. This is a stark contrast to the process of maturity outlined in verses 2-4, where trials develop perseverance that matures into perfection. James implies his readers must head in one of two directions, either down the path of trial to perfection or the path of desire to death.

1:16 Don't be deceived, my dear brothers. 1:17 Every good and perfect gift is from above, coming down from the Father of the heavenly lights, who does not change like shifting shadows.

Thus, the individual, not God, is responsible for temptation. The idea that God leads one to sin is deception. God's nature prohibits him from doing evil toward humanity. He is consistent in giving only good and perfect gifts. James uses the metaphor of "lights" for the consistent goodness of God. He is the Father of lights because he created the heavenly lights – sun, moon, and stars – in the beginning (Genesis 1:14-19; Psalm 136:7). These lights are the first of his good and perfect gifts. However, the light from these heavenly bodies changes from an earthly point of view. The moon has its phases. Sometimes the planets and stars cannot be seen. Even the sun is sometimes eclipsed. By contrast, the Giver of light is not changeable like the gift. God's goodness always shines on his people. "God is light; in him there is no darkness at all" (1 John 1:5).

This reference to heavenly bodies may also be James's version of the later Shakespearean quote: "The fault . . . is not in our stars, but in ourselves . . . ." It is not fate or astrology that guides human lives; it is a God whose nature is unchangeably good. If we are tempted, the fault is not his, but ours.

1:18 He chose to give us birth through the word of truth,

God does not leave our destiny to chance. He intentionally planned to give us new birth. Just as he created the stars in the beginning and so is "the Father of lights," so now he has chosen to begin a new creation by "giving us birth through the word of truth."[5] "Word of truth" may refer to the creative word that made humans in the beginning ("Let us make man in our image," Genesis 1:26), to the truth of the gospel that gives new birth (1 Corinthians 4:15), or, most likely, to Jesus the Word (John 1:1) and the truth (John 14:6) who brings new life.

that we might be a kind of firstfruits of all he created.

Those who have been born anew are "firstfruits" (ἀπαρχή, *aparchē*) of a new creation (cf. the note on 2 Thessalonians 2:13 in the NIV). In the Old Testament, the first crops were dedicated to God in sacrifice (Exodus 23:16; Leviticus 2:12). Those who are born through the word of truth also present themselves as sacrifices to God (cf. Romans 12:1). "Firstfruits" might also imply that those born anew are a preview of the new creation (cf. Romans 8:22-23). This birth to life contrasts with the birth of sin to death (v. 15).

Section Summary and Application:

When struggling with temptation, particularly with one that has often overpowered us, it is easy to try to shift the blame to others, to our social environment, to the devil, or

---

[5]I believe James is speaking of the new creation, however see L.E. Elliott-Binns, "James 1:18: Creation or Redemption?", *New Testament Studies* 3 (1956), 148-161, who argues that these verses refer to the original creation, not to redemption as second creation.

even to God. One form this has recently taken is to root our behavior, even our sins, in our genetic code. We are not to blame, because "God made us this way." James will not allow this shift in responsibility. There is no one to blame for temptation and sin but ourselves.

God does not tempt. He gives only good gifts. His consistent goodness shines for all to see. The greatest gift of all is the new birth we experienced through his Son. Although we are subject to temptation and sin, by God's help we can overcome every trial and temptation that comes our way and receive the promised crown of life.

VI. SPEAKING, LISTENING, DOING (1:19-27)

[19]My dear brothers, take note of this: Everyone should be quick to listen, slow to speak and slow to become angry, [20]for man's anger does not bring about the righteous life that God desires. [21]Therefore, get rid of all moral filth and the evil that is so prevalent and humbly accept the word planted in you, which can save you.

[22]Do not merely listen to the word, and so deceive yourselves. Do what it says. [23]Anyone who listens to the word but does not do what it says is like a man who looks at his face in a mirror [24]and, after looking at himself, goes away and immediately forgets what he looks like. [25]But the man who looks intently into the perfect law that gives freedom, and continues to do this, not forgetting what he has heard, but doing it — he will be blessed in what he does.

[26]If anyone considers himself religious and yet does not keep a tight rein on his tongue, he deceives himself and his religion is worthless. [27]Religion that God our Father accepts as pure and faultless is this: to look after orphans and widows in their distress and to keep oneself from being polluted by the world.

1:19 My dear brothers, take note of this: Everyone should be quick to listen, slow to speak and slow to become angry,

Warnings about hasty speech are found throughout the wisdom books of the Old Testament (Proverbs 10:14; 15:1; 17:27-28; 29:20; Ecclesiastes 7:9) as well as in writings of the Greek and Roman moral philosophers. The Stoic philosopher Seneca, for example, sees brevity of speech as a sign of character. To control speech is to control self. Elaborate speech is immodest. Silence, on the other hand, prevents one from error.[6] The modern proverb, "Better to keep your mouth shut and be thought a fool than to open it and remove all doubt," may be part of what James has in mind here.

James ties his warning against hasty speech with hearing (a preview of vv. 22-25) and to anger. Some suggest this is a warning against setting oneself up as a teacher (thus quick to listen to and slow to speak the "word of truth," v. 18), a theme James returns to in 3:1-12. More likely it is a caution against rash and angry words in general.

1:20 for man's anger does not bring about the righteous life that God desires.

There is a place for righteous anger, but Jesus taught that those quick to speak angry words are in danger of judgment from God (Matthew 5:21-26). "Righteous indignation" is rarely completely righteous. This may be what James means by anger not bringing about "the righteousness life that God desires." In other words, anger is not the right thing, the thing God approves.

However, these words may mean that anger does not hasten the judgment of God against evil. Christians see injustice in the world and even suffer unjustly themselves. However, if they lash out with angry words against evil, it may make them

---

[6]For more on silence and speech in the ancient world, see Luke Timothy Johnson, "Taciturnity and True Religion," in David L. Balch, ed., *Greeks, Romans, and Christians: Essays in Honor of Abraham J. Mahlherbe* (Minneapolis: Fortress Press, 1990), pp. 330-339.

feel better but does not in itself bring justice. They should not resign themselves to evil, nor merely complain at it, but should wait patiently for the Lord to return and execute justice (James 5:7).

1:21 Therefore, get rid of all moral filth and the evil that is so prevalent

Instead of being angry, Christians should rid their lives of evil. "Get rid" is actually a metaphor of taking off one set of clothes and putting on another. Thus, Christians are to put off the filthy clothes of hasty speech, anger, and all kinds of evil and to put on Christ. This metaphor of "take off" and "put on" occurs in many places in the New Testament and may refer to the change of life that takes place in baptism (Romans 13:12; Ephesians 4:22-25; Colossians 3:8; Hebrews 12:1; 1 Peter 2:1). It is another way of speaking of that new birth and creation that God gives (see v. 18).

and humbly accept the word planted in you,

James mixes his metaphors by changing from putting off evil like clothing to receiving the implanted word. The term "implanted" (ἔμφυτον, *emphyton*), can mean "innate" in other contexts. Here the word is obviously not innately natural in the Christian but must be received or accepted from God. In the parable of the sower (Mark 4:3-20), Jesus speaks of the word as planted seed (cf. 1 Corinthians 3:6). James urges his readers to be good soil, that is, to have good hearts that receive the word with humility (cf. 1 Thessalonians 2:13). To accept the word means one allows it to govern all of life.

which can save you.

James says the word is powerful enough to save (cf. Romans 1:16; 1 Corinthians 1:18). That word saves by continuing to transform their lives, making them truly the firstfruits of a new creation (v. 18). Clearly James is not just a moralist who urges his readers to be better through their own power. It is God through his word who empowers them to control their speech and anger. It is he who gives them birth through the word.

1:22 Do not merely listen to the word, and so deceive yourselves. Do what it says.

They must be quick to listen to the word, but listening is not enough. Action is required (cf. Romans 2:13). James has an extended comparison between the mere listener (literally, listener "alone," μόνον, *monon*, the same word used in 2:24 of faith alone) and the doer.

1:23 Anyone who listens to the word but does not do what it says is like a man who looks at his face in a mirror

The heart of the comparison is the mirror analogy.[7] The mere hearer, who is self-deceived, sees his natural face in a mirror and goes away and forgets what he looks like. The doer gazes into the law of liberty, remains there, does not forget, and so is blessed.

Mirrors in the ancient world were of polished metal and thus did not give as clear a reflection as modern mirrors. However, as with mirrors today, their main function was to inspect and improve personal appearance. A mirror allows a person to know his physical appearance and improve it. Ancient moral philosophers, such as Plutarch, used the cosmetic function of mirrors as an analogy for moral improvement. As one gazes in a mirror to see and correct physical imperfections, so one gazes into moral examples to see ethical faults and correct them.

1:24 and, after looking at himself, goes away and immediately forgets what he looks like.

James uses the mirror as an example in a similar way. If you look in a mirror, see a smudge on your face or your hair out of place, and do nothing to improve your appearance,

---

[7]See Luke Timothy Johnson, "The Mirror of Remembrance, James 1:22-25," *Catholic Biblical Quarterly* 50 (1988), 632-645.

then you have forgotten what you should look like or are self-deceived, believing you are attractive as you are with no room for improvement. In the same way, one who hears the word but does not do it has forgotten the ethical demands of the word and has deceived himself into thinking he is already perfect.

1:25 But the man who looks intently into the perfect law that gives freedom,

One the other hand, the doer looks into "the perfect law that gives freedom." Here clearly James is talking about more than a physical mirror. It is the law one gazes into. "Law" is an important word for James. He uses it here for the first time. To understand his use of "law" requires avoiding the misconceptions many Christians have concerning the word. James is no legalist. He does not believe Christians are saved by law rather than grace. However, his witness is consistent with that of all biblical writers, including Paul: "the law is good" (Romans 7:16). James even says it is perfect, one of the perfect gifts that the Father of lights gives (James 1:17). James reflects the praise for the law in Psalm 119 and other Old Testament passages as well as the teaching of Jesus who came not to abolish the law but to fulfill it (Matthew 5:17).

Even more startling to many contemporary Christians, James calls it the law of freedom (see also James 2:12). Law and freedom seem completely antithetical to some. To James, doing the law brings true freedom. But what does James mean by "the law?" In context it is synonymous with "the word of truth" that gives new birth (v. 18) and the implanted word that saves (v. 21). That word is ultimately Jesus himself (John 1:1) and, in a secondary sense, the saving word about Jesus, the gospel. So, while Paul sometimes contrasts law and gospel, to James the law that brings freedom *is* the gospel.

and continues to do this, not forgetting what he has heard, but doing it — he will be blessed in what he does.

The gospel not only saves, but it teaches how one should

behave as a saved person. Or as James would say, the law brings freedom from sin but also serves as a mirror of the soul, showing areas where improvement is needed. The one who does the word (that is, obeys the gospel), gazes into the law, does not forget what he sees, but changes his life accordingly. Such a doer is blessed by God, as Jesus himself said, "Blessed rather are those who hear the word of God and obey it" (Luke 11:28; see also Matthew 7:24-27).

It is interesting to compare the mirror analogy in James with a similar analogy from Paul. "And we, who with unveiled faces all reflect the Lord's glory, are being transformed into his likeness with ever-increasing glory, which comes from the Lord, who is the Spirit" (2 Corinthians 3:18). Although the word "mirror" is not used in this passage, the idea of reflection implies it (see NRSV "as though reflected in a mirror"). To Paul, the mirror is the Lord's glory or the Lord himself who, through the Spirit, morally transforms Christians into his likeness. In Paul, the Christian is passive; he is transformed by the mirror. In James, the Christian is active; he must do what he sees in the law of freedom. This is not a contradiction between Paul and James but a difference in emphasis between them. Paul also calls for an active faith, and James believes in salvation by grace.

1:26 If anyone considers himself religious and yet does not keep a tight rein on his tongue, he deceives himself and his religion is worthless.

That active response of faith is given concrete meaning in self-control and compassion for those in need. The mere hearer may deceive himself into thinking he is religious. "Religious" (θρησκός, *thrēskos*) has the same connotation in Greek as in English. It can refer to one who has a genuine walk with God or to one who merely keeps outward rituals. Such religion is worthless if one does not control his speech. Reining in the tongue is a common metaphor in the ancient world for self-control (James returns to it in 3:3-8). As discussed above (vs. 19), to be slow to speak is a sign of character.

Self-proclaimed religion is no good unless followed by action. One should be slow to talk the talk but quick to walk the walk.

1:27 Religion that God our Father accepts as pure and faultless is this:

That walk is to follow the steps of Jesus in helping the downtrodden. Such religion is pure (καθαρός, *katharos*) and faultless (ἀμίαντος, *amiantos*), words associated with ceremonial cleanness in the Old Testament (Genesis 7:2; 8:20; Leviticus 4:12; 7:19; 11:32; 15:13; Numbers 8:7; Deuteronomy 12:15). Jesus takes that concern for ceremonial cleanness and ties it to a concern for those in need: "But give what is inside the dish to the poor, and everything will be clean for you" (Luke 11:41). That is the genuine religion that God approves, a religion that is more than outward ritual and ceremony (cf. Micah 6:7-8). True religion to James (as well as to Jesus) is not found in religious language or ritual alone but in selfless acts of service.

to look after orphans and widows in their distress

Those singled out for help are orphans and widows. In the ancient world, unwanted children were often abandoned to die. Orphans were rarely cared for by the state or by private foundations. Without family, on their own, they were certainly in distress. Women in the ancient world seldom worked outside the home. An unmarried woman depended solely on her parents for support; a married woman, solely on her husband. A widow without children or with children who would not support her was doomed to poverty. Thus, orphans and widows are singled out by the Old Testament as protected by God and as proper objects for compassion and assistance (Deuteronomy 10:18; 14:28-29; 16:11; 24:17; 26:12; Jeremiah 22:3; Zechariah 7:8-10; Malachi 3:5; cf. Acts 6:1; 1 Timothy 5:16). Of course, James does not intend to limit compassion to only widows and orphans. All in need are our neighbors.

and to keep oneself from being polluted by the world.

True religion is shown by care for those in distress but also by keeping oneself unstained (ἄσπιλος, *aspilos*) by the world. This is such an abrupt shift from compassion that some scholars suggest the reading from a Greek papyrus is the correct one: ". . . to look after widows and orphans and to protect them from the world."[8] However, the majority of manuscripts have "keep oneself from being polluted by the world" as in the NIV. This is not such an abrupt shift after all, since worldliness to James includes greed, pride, and an arrogance toward the poor (James 2:1-13; 4:1-12). Giving generously to those in need is a challenge to worldly standards of worth and success.

Section Summary and Application:

This discussion of hearing and doing serves as a corrective to the cheap grace practiced by many in the church today. Salvation by grace does not mean that moral standards are lower for Christians. Indeed, it is Jesus who calls his disciples to a higher righteousness (Matthew 5:20). In James's day, as well as ours, there were those who deceived themselves into thinking they were saved because they had heard the gracious words of salvation. James reminds them that grace requires an active response. Such a response includes control of our speech, care for those in need, and rejection of the standards of the world.

---

[8]David J. Roberts III, "The Definition of 'Pure Religion' in James 1:27," *The Expository Times* 83 (April 1972), 215-216, argues that this is the original reading in the text of James. However, most scholars disagree. For a rebuttal of Roberts, see Bruce C. Johanson, "The Definition of 'Pure Religion' in James 1:27 Reconsidered," *The Expository Times* 84 (January 1973), 118-119.

JAMES 2

VII. JUDGING BY APPEARANCE (2:1-13)

A. FAVORITISM (2:1-7)

¹My brothers, as believers in our glorious Lord Jesus Christ, don't show favoritism. ²Suppose a man comes into your meeting wearing a gold ring and fine clothes, and a poor man in shabby clothes also comes in. ³If you show special attention to the man wearing fine clothes and say, "Here's a good seat for you," but say to the poor man, "You stand there" or "Sit on the floor by my feet," ⁴have you not discriminated among yourselves and become judges with evil thoughts?

⁵Listen, my dear brothers: Has not God chosen those who are poor in the eyes of the world to be rich in faith and to inherit the kingdom he promised those who love him? ⁶But you have insulted the poor. Is it not the rich who are exploiting you? Are they not the ones who are dragging you into court? ⁷Are they not the ones who are slandering the noble name of him to whom you belong?

This section is in the form of a diatribe, an ancient literary style used particularly in discussions of morality. Diatribe is usually a polemic, a strong denunciation against immoral actions. It involves a lively style characterized by direct address of the readers, a dialogue with an imaginary opponent, and striking imaginary examples. It was a style associated with schools and learning, especially the learning of morality.[1] Here James schools his readers against the deadly effects of favoritism.

2:1 My brothers, as believers in our glorious Lord Jesus Christ,

He begins his strong warning against favoritism with a gentle introduction, "my brothers" (later, in v. 5, "my dear brothers"). His harsh words are tempered by this warm greeting. James is no arrogant, superior teacher, but a loving shepherd who cares enough for his flock to alert them to the subtle dangers of partiality. His repeated use of "brothers" also reminds them of the true basis of their relationship to one another. Christians do not choose their brothers because they are rich, powerful, or good looking. All are chosen by grace to be children of God. That is what makes them brothers. If the relationship is made by God, the brothers must not break it through partiality and prejudice.

don't show favoritism.

James says the brothers cannot have faith in Jesus and show favoritism. The term "favoritism" or "partiality" (προσω-πολημψία, *prosōpolēmpsia*) comes from the Greek root for "face" (πρόσωπον, *prosōpon*). Favoritism is judging others based on appearance, that is, at face value. It reflects the Hebrew idiom "to lift up the face," that is, to show favor to someone. What is condemned here is injustice, preferring the rich to the poor and the powerful to the helpless. James ended the last chapter by calling for the truly religious to care for orphans and widows. Here he says one cannot genuinely care for the poor while being partial to the rich.

Partiality, that is, judging appearance instead of the heart, is directly contrary to the character of God. "For the Lord your God is God of gods and Lord of lords, the great God, mighty and awesome, who shows no partiality and accepts no

---

[1]Stanley Kent Stowers, *The Diatribe and Paul's Letter to the Romans* (Chico, CA: Scholars Press, 1981), pp. 7-78.

bribes. He defends the cause of the fatherless and the widow, and loves the alien, giving him food and clothing" (Deuteronomy 10:17-18). To have faith in Jesus Christ, the Lord of glory, means following the example of Jesus who brought good news to the poor (Luke 4:18). It means imitating the character of this glorious, impartial, generous God. It means Christians will not be fooled by the apparent glory of the rich but will recognize the one is truly glorious. It also means caring for orphans and widows as God himself does, thus tying this section on partiality to the pure religion discussed in 1:27. To fail to care for the poor is to be partial toward the rich.

The impartial and just nature of God is a leading theme of the New Testament. Peter tells Cornelius that God does not show favoritism but accepts those who fear him from every nation (Acts 10:34-35). Paul agrees that salvation is for Jew and Gentile, since "God does not show favoritism" (Romans 2:11). Masters are to treat their slaves well because they have a Master in heaven who shows no favoritism (Ephesians 6:9). Slaves who do wrong will be punished by the Lord Christ, without favoritism (Colossians 3:25). Even when the enemies of Jesus seek to trap him, they have to admit he is impartial, literally, that he does not "see people's faces" (Mark 12:14).

Both Testaments are consistently witness that God and Christ do not play favorites. They do not prefer rich to poor, master to slave, or even Jew to Gentile. They judge fairly, by looking at the heart. Those who claim Jesus Christ as their Lord must also judge fairly and not at face value. "Do not pervert justice; do not show partiality to the poor or favoritism to the great, but judge your neighbor fairly" (Leviticus 19:15).

2:2 Suppose a man comes into your meeting wearing a gold ring and fine clothes, and a poor man in shabby clothes also comes in.

James could have ended his admonition with this bare prohibition of favoritism. However, he puts teeth into it with a hypothetical example. He talks of two men who come into the "meeting." The Greek word here is συναγωγή, "synagogue," an unusual term for a Christian assembly. It might point to an early date for James, a time when Christianity was still thought of as merely a sect of Judaism. This meeting may be a worship assembly or may reflect a meeting for judging between Christians.

2:3 If you show special attention to the man wearing fine clothes and say, "Here's a good seat for you," but say to the poor man, "You stand there" or "Sit on the floor by my feet,"

If a worship assembly is the setting, the example is one of treating people differently ("discriminated among yourselves," v. 4) on the basis of appearance alone. A visitor enters who possibly is a non-Christian but probably a new convert or a Christian from another church, since the distinction made is "among yourselves" (v. 4). He wears a gold ring, a sign of both wealth and position, and bright, splendid clothes. Here is a man of refinement who oozes power, money, and success. Some might think this is the kind of affluent professional person who can provide the social and financial stability the church needs. He is greeted effusively and given a good seat (the Greek can also mean, "have a seat, please"). In the meantime, a man in filthy rags slips in and is told to stand or (literally in Greek) to "sit under my footstool." This is mockery. He can sit on the floor or hide under the footstool or (best of all) just leave. The church wants this man simply to disappear.

It may be, however, that the setting James has in mind is not a worship assembly but an assembly where the church is settling a dispute between members (see Matthew 18:15-20; 1 Corinthians 5:3-5; 6:1-8; 1 Timothy 5:19-24). If so, "have you not discriminated among yourselves and become judges with evil thoughts" (v. 4) means they are guilty not just of social but legal discrimination. The richly dressed man is shown preference by being allowed to sit (in Rabbinical courts, the parties to the case usually stood). The shabbily dressed man must stand or even grovel ("under my footstool") before the judges.² The case, therefore, is decided by the church before testimony is given. They have become evil because they do not judge fairly, a direct violation of the prohibition of Leviticus 19:15.

2:4 have you not discriminated among yourselves and become judges with evil thoughts?

In either case, a grievous sin is committed because Christians are judging others by the world's standards, not by God's. A clear choice is given. The world's measurement is the opposite of God's. The phrase, "discriminated (διακρίνω, *diakrinō*) among yourselves" points not only to division in the church but to division in the heart; it can be translated, "divided within yourselves." Trying to hold to faith in Jesus and the standards of the world at the same time is an impossible task. Like doubt in prayer, it makes one "double-minded" (James 1:8)

2:5 Listen, my dear brothers: Has not God chosen those who are poor in the eyes of the world to be rich in faith and to inherit the kingdom he promised those who love him?

James urges his brothers to be consistent. To have faith in Jesus is to judge by his standards. They must listen to the difficult message that God chooses those they would not choose, those poor (πτωχός, *ptōchos*) in the eyes of the world (see 1 Corinthians 1:27-28). It is the poor who will inherit the kingdom of God (Luke 6:20). Again, as in 1:9-11, God's power reverses earthly status; the poor and lowly are exalted, and the rich and powerful are brought low. True religion is to help widows and orphans, not to grovel before the rich. Christians must keep themselves from being polluted by worldly measurements of value (James 1:27).

2:6 But you have insulted the poor. Is it not the rich who are

---

²Roy Bowen Ward, "Partiality in the Assembly: James 2:2-4," *Harvard Theological Review* 62 (1969), 87-97.

exploiting you? Are they not the ones who are dragging you into court?

Discriminating against the poor goes against the very nature of the God who is no respecter of persons. To James, it also makes no practical sense. Why insult (ἀτιμάζω, *atimazō*, "dishonor") the poor, when they are loved by God? Why fawn over and toady to the rich, when they are the ones who oppress Christians? Here James probably does not have rich Christians in mind but those wealthy and powerful persecutors of the church. Rich owners exploit powerless workers (see James 5:3-6). They use the legal system to cheat the poor.

2:7 Are they not the ones who are slandering the noble name of him to whom you belong?

They even blaspheme the name of Christ to whom Christians belong (in Greek, "the noble (καλός, *kalos*) name called over you"). These poor had been baptized in the name of Jesus (Acts 2:38; 10:48; 19:5; 1 Corinthians 6:11) and carried his name with them (Revelation 2:13). The rich cause them to suffer because the poor bear this name (Acts 5:41; 1 Peter 4:14). Why then should Christians prefer the rich either inside or outside the church?

The basic question behind their attitude toward the rich is this: "Who controls the world?" If the rich really are in charge, then poor Christians must keep their proper place if they are to survive. Deference must be shown to those who pay them wages. Workers should be servile, always giving preference to the rich who hold their means of livelihood in their hands. Rich and powerful patrons could help the church in its mission. Even if the rich could not be won over to help the church, at least honoring them might allow Christians to escape being dragged away to jail. Not to favor the rich may have consequences — oppression, imprisonment, and slander. But James has already said that such trials are pure joy that end in the perfection of the believers (James 1:2-4).

However, if Christ is truly the glorious Lord of the world, then he, not the rich, should be served. Indeed, to serve the rich is to side with those who curse Jesus. It puts one on the side of Satan, not God. The one who claims to follow the glorious Lord Jesus and then shows favoritism to the rich is guilty of having a divided allegiance. He is like the double-minded man (James 1:7-8). He wants to do the impossible, to befriend God and the world (James 4:4).

But it is not enough to avoid preferring the rich; one must also not despise the poor (Proverbs 14:21). This is what James accuses them of doing (v. 6). He has gone beyond the specific example above to a wider application. It is not just a matter of where poor and rich should sit in the assembly but an overall prejudice for the rich and against the poor that James condemns. In the ancient world, honor and shame were all-important concepts. God has honored the poor. Christians must not shame them.

B. THE ROYAL LAW (2:8-13)

⁸**If you really keep the royal law found in Scripture, "Love your neighbor as yourself,"ᵃ you are doing right. ⁹But if you show favoritism, you sin and are convicted by the law as lawbreakers. ¹⁰For whoever keeps the whole law and yet stumbles at just one point is guilty of breaking all of it. ¹¹For he who said, "Do not commit adultery,"ᵇ also said, "Do not murder."ᶜ If you do not commit adultery but do commit murder, you have become a lawbreaker.**

¹²Speak and act as those who are going to be judged by the law that gives freedom, ¹³because judgment without mercy will be shown to anyone who has not been merciful. Mercy triumphs over judgment!

ᵃ*8* Lev. 19:18   ᵇ*11* Exodus 20:14; Deut. 5:18   ᶜ*11* Exodus 20:13; Deut. 5:17

2:8 If you really keep the royal law found in Scripture, "Love your neighbor as yourself," you are doing right.

Favoritism is more than foolish; it is sin. One who believes in the Lord Jesus commits himself to keep the law of Christ, specifically the royal law to love (ἀγαπάω, *agapaō*) neighbor as self. This is a royal law because it comes from the King and is the law of the kingdom the poor will inherit (v. 5). "Royal" also implies it is a supreme principle, not a petty regulation. Love of neighbor is an Old Testament law (Leviticus 19:18), occurring in the context of a prohibition against favoritism (Leviticus 19:15). Jesus calls it the second great commandment, love for God being first (Matthew 19:19; 22:39). Paul says love of neighbor sums up all the commandments (Romans 13:9; Galatians 5:14).

2:9 But if you show favoritism, you sin and are convicted by the law as lawbreakers.

Those claiming to keep the law of love while showing favoritism may have thought they could choose their neighbors. The neighbor was someone like themselves or someone they wished to imitate, one with fine clothes, gold rings, and power. Jesus answers the question, "Who is my neighbor?", by telling the story of the Good Samaritan (Luke 10:25-37). No doubt the priest and the Levite who passed by the wounded man might have helped him if they had believed he was wealthy and prominent. However, all they knew was that he was one in need. It was the Samaritan who actively showed mercy to this stranger and proved to be his neighbor. The point is clear: Christians must be neighbors to anyone in need. To withhold assistance on the basis of appearance is to break the law of love.

2:10 For whoever keeps the whole law and yet stumbles at just one point is guilty of breaking all of it.

Partiality or favoritism violates the law, "Love your neighbor as yourself," and so makes one guilty of breaking the whole law. The idea that breaking a single law makes one guilty of breaking all of it was a common one in Stoic philosophy and also among certain Jewish rabbis.[3] At first, such a

---

[3]Marjorie O'Rourke Boyle, "The Stoic Paradox of James 2:10," *New Testament Studies* 31 (1985), 611-617.

principle makes James look like the worst of legalists, demanding perfection from his readers. It seems he equates all commands, not making the distinction Jesus did between lesser and more important laws (Matthew 23:23-24). But this is a misunderstanding of James.

2:11 For he who said, "Do not commit adultery," also said, "Do not murder." If you do not commit adultery but do commit murder, you have become a lawbreaker.

In context, the purpose for citing the principle of "break one law, break all" is to combat the legalism of those who view favoritism as a "little" sin. They claim to follow Christ and keep his laws. They avoid the "big" sins, adultery and murder, sins that Jesus himself clearly condemned (Matthew 5:21, 27; 19:18; Mark 10:18; Luke 18:20), but they ignore another command from the same Lawgiver, the command to avoid favoritism. They are so self-deceived that they cannot see that favoritism is a violation of the command to love their neighbor. It is no slight imperfection but a sin as bad as adultery and murder.

What James promotes is not legalism but consistency between a claimed faith and visible actions. He knows that the point of the royal law is to show obedience to the King who loves us, not just to be better than others in keeping a list of commands. He battles the hypocrisy of those who claim faith in Jesus on the basis of a partial obedience, but who reject the heart of Jesus who loves the downtrodden. One cannot obey the law without imitating the Lawgiver. Love of neighbor is not just one rule among many. It is a reflection of the character of God.

2:12 Speak and act as those who are going to be judged by the law that gives freedom,

Believers should judge others as they wish to be judged (Matthew 7:1-2). They judged the two men who entered their meeting on outward appearance. They do not want to be judged that way by God. No one wants to be judged by a harsh, stringent law but by "the law that gives freedom." To James, the true purpose of the law is not to chain the evildoer but to set him free. The law of Christ gives freedom from sin but also sets one free from selfishness. It frees from fawning over the rich to gain their influence. It frees from the oppression from the rich, turning trials into joy. It frees one to love those who are unlovable by worldly standards. It frees from the constant competition and self-promotion society takes for granted.

2:13 because judgment without mercy will be shown to anyone who has not been merciful. Mercy triumphs over judgment!

That law of freedom is also a law of mercy. All want God to judge them not based on their outward appearance, or wealth, or even on their ability to keep his law perfectly. They want mercy. Christians have received mercy and forgiveness through the cross. In turn, they must show not just impartiality but mercy in dealing with others. In the hypothetical example above, some had spoken harshly to the poor man and treated him badly in the assembly. Instead, they must speak and act as those who desire mercy. There is an echo here of the parable of the unmerciful servant (Matthew 18:21-35). The one who shows no mercy will receive none. Or to put it positively, in the words of Jesus, "Blessed are the merciful, for they will be shown mercy" (Matthew 5:7).

James' scathing denunciation of favoritism is meant to help, not to harm his beloved brothers. In this section, he forces his readers to look intently into the mirror of the law of liberty (James 1:25). In that mirror, they see themselves as they really are, self-deceived hypocrites who claim faith in Jesus but who fail the test of love for those in need. Such a sight is shocking and painful. After seeing themselves, they have a choice. They can, with God's grace, repent of their favoritism by showing acts of mercy to the needy. Or they can forget what they have seen and so cut themselves off from God's mercy.

Section Summary and Application:

The very idea that Christians can hold faith in Christ and then judge people by such worldly standards is absurd. To do so makes us judges with evil thoughts. James clearly confronts our human tendency to prefer those outwardly successful to those on the margins of society. His example hits home. This kind of partiality can be seen in many churches and many hearts today.

God's standards challenge our common sense ideas of how the church should be. They call for conversion, for complete reversal of the way we judge others and do church. If the church should target anyone, it is not the influential opinion leaders of the community, but the poor who need to hear good news. Perhaps one reason churches fail to grow today is that we try to build churches on those who think they are self-sufficient, instead of on those in need.

To disassociate with the poor is to cut oneself off from those who are God's chosen. It is to align ourselves with those who blaspheme Christ. It is a sin as bad as murder or adultery. It places us in danger of judgment without mercy because we have failed to show mercy.

VIII. FAITH THAT WORKS (2:14-26)

A. FAITH WITHOUT WORKS (2:14-17)

¹⁴What good is it, my brothers, if a man claims to have faith but has no deeds? Can such faith save him? ¹⁵Suppose a brother or sister is without clothes and daily food. ¹⁶If one of you says to him, "Go, I wish you well; keep warm and well fed," but does nothing about his physical needs, what good is it? ¹⁷In the same way, faith by itself, if it is not accompanied by action, is dead.

As in the section above, James here condemns those who claim faith but do not put their faith into practice by caring for others. This is one of the best known and most often misunderstood sections in James. Since the early Christian centuries, some have seen a contradiction (or, at least, a difference in emphasis) between Paul who says one is saved by faith without works and James who clearly says faith without works cannot save. We will see below that there is no contradiction between James and Paul. Each believes one is saved by grace through faith, a faith shown by actions.

James has a different purpose for writing about faith and works than Paul has in Galatians. His purpose is pastoral. He wants to convince Christians that half-hearted ("double-minded") faith is no true faith at all. Such faith can only be claimed, not shown. Such faith is no good. It makes no difference in one's life or in the lives of others. It cannot save. James condemns such "faith" as mere intellectual agreement to a set of doctrines without a change of life. He fights the idea that salvation by faith is purely personal, that it does not require obligation to others and does not lead to compassion for the needy. Even this early in the history of the church, there were uninvolved church members, considering themselves religious (James 1:26), sure they were saved by faith but living like the world around them. This is a false view of faith.

2:14 What good is it, my brothers, if a man claims to have faith but has no deeds? Can such faith save him?

True faith moves one to true religion: to care for orphans and widows (James 1:27) and to love neighbor as self (James 2:8). James shows the inadequacy of a merely claimed faith by the use of another powerful hypothetical example. Someone who is more than a neighbor, a brother or sister in Christ, comes to you in obvious need of the bare necessities of life. What should you do?

2:15 Suppose a brother or sister is without clothes and daily food. 2:16 If one of you says to him, "Go, I wish you well; keep warm and well fed," but does nothing about his physical needs, what good is it?

If your faith is merely verbal, you greet him piously, "I wish you well" (literally, "go in peace," the typical biblical greeting, cf. Judges 18:6; 1 Samuel 1:17; 20:42; 29:7; 2 Samuel 15:9; 2 Kings 5:19; Mark 5:34; Luke 7:50; Acts 16:36). You wish him no harm and even hope he finds warmth and food. Yet such a greeting is actually a dismissal. The contemporary equivalent would be, "Good-by and good luck." You feel uncomfortable in the presence of the needy, so you usher them out quickly with religious clichés. But if one is cold and hungry, what good are pious platitudes? None at all. Those in need go away just as cold and hungry as they came.

2:17 In the same way, faith by itself, if it is not accompanied by action, is dead.

The very idea that anyone with an ounce of human kindness could turn away such needy people is beyond comprehension. What is more astounding is that they can turn them away while claiming to be people of faith. Turning a needy brother or sister away is the direct opposite of the practice of the first church in Jerusalem. "They shared everything they had" so "there were no needy persons among them" (Acts 4:32, 34). By contrast, it is empty sentimentality to think that sympathetic feelings are enough to help others. Such faith does the needy no good. It is a dead faith, that is, no faith at all. In this instance a dead faith spreads death. The needy starve in the presence of such "faith."

Yet some are so self-deceived, they can withhold assistance from the needy and still think they are faithfully following God and the Lord Jesus. This hypocrisy and self-deception are not new. Even in the Old Testament, there were many who thought they were right with God because they believed the right thing and worshipped correctly, while they oppressed and neglected the poor. God reminded them that true worship is to feed the hungry, shelter the homeless, and clothe the naked (Isaiah 58:6-10).

Jesus himself warns that when the Son of Man comes, some will call him Lord and yet be cast into eternal fire. Why?

"For I was hungry and you gave me nothing to eat, I was thirsty and you gave me nothing to drink, I was a stranger and you did not invite me in, I needed clothes and you did not clothe me, I was sick and in prison and you did not look after me" (Matthew 25:42-43). When did they fail to help Jesus? "I tell you the truth, whatever you did not do for the least of these, you did not do it for me" (Matthew 25:45). In the passage on the last day from the Sermon on the Mount, Jesus says, "Not everyone who says to me, 'Lord, Lord,' will enter the kingdom of heaven, but only he who does the will of my Father who is in heaven" (Matthew 7:21). James makes the same point in his example; to claim faith while dismissing the needy is not doing God's will. It is not genuine faith. It only leads to death.

B. FAITH WITH WORKS (2:18-26)

[18]But someone will say, "You have faith; I have deeds."

Show me your faith without deeds, and I will show you my faith by what I do. [19]You believe that there is one God. Good! Even the demons believe that — and shudder.

[20]You foolish man, do you want evidence that faith without deeds is useless[a]? [21]Was not our ancestor Abraham considered righteous for what he did when he offered his son Isaac on the altar? [22]You see that his faith and his actions were working together, and his faith was made complete by what he did. [23]And the scripture was fulfilled that says, "Abraham believed God, and it was credited to him as righteousness,"[b] and he was called God's friend. [24]You see that a person is justified by what he does and not by faith alone.

[25]In the same way, was not even Rahab the prostitute considered righteous for what she did when she gave lodging to the spies and sent them off in a different direction? [26]As the body without the spirit is dead, so faith without deeds is dead.

[a]*20* Some early manuscripts *dead*   [b]*23* Gen. 15:6

2:18 But someone will say, "You have faith; I have deeds."

What is clear in the hypothetical example of verses 15-16 is a general principle for James; there is a necessary unity between action and attitude. An imaginary opponent objects to this unity: "You have faith; I have deeds."[4] The thrust of this objection is that faith and deeds can be separated; some are better at one, some at the other. In this view, the church has "believers" and "doers." Both are necessary, argues this opponent, and each should tolerate the other.

Show me your faith without deeds, and I will show you my faith by what I do.

James will have none of this separation. An unseen faith is no faith at all. Thus, "Show me your faith without deeds," is an ironic statement. It is an impossible request. Faith cannot be seen without action. Faith is seen only in deeds of love and compassion. It is always wrong to separate faith and deeds.

This separation has led to much misunderstanding throughout Christian history. Some have misunderstood Paul's contention that one is saved by faith apart from the works of the Law, to mean that one is saved by faith alone without that faith being shown in actions. However, in Galatians, where he most clearly fights salvation through

---

[4]Verse 18 is a difficult passage that has provoked many interpretations from commentators. The problem is that biblical Greek has no quotation marks. Thus it is up to the reader to infer from context whether there is a quotation and where the quotation begins and ends. "But someone will say . . ." makes it clear that James is introducing a quotation. If the quotation extends throughout verse 18 ("You have faith; I have deeds. Show me your faith without deeds and I will show you my faith by what I do."), then this someone is agreeing with James that deeds show faith. More likely, as in the NIV, the quotation is only the first sentence ("You have faith; I have deeds.") which means the someone disagrees with James' position and James' reply is "Show me your faith . . . ." This second possibility with an imaginary objector is more in line with the diatribe form that James is using. For more on this question see Scot McKnight, "James 2:18a: The Unidentifiable Interlocutor," *Westminster Theological Journal* 52 (1990), 355-364.

works of the Law, Paul summarizes his position by saying, "For in Christ Jesus neither circumcision nor uncircumcision has any value. The only thing that counts is faith expressing itself through love" (Galatians 5:6). The words translated "expressing itself" is the verb form of the word "work" or "deed," the same word James uses. Thus Paul, like James, does not separate faith from action. Like James, Paul uses phrases like "your work produced by faith" (1 Thessalonians 1:3) and "every act prompted by your faith" (2 Thessalonians 1:11).

One is correct, then, to deny the doctrine of "faith only" in the sense of salvation by faith apart from the deeds of faith. James later will specifically refute justification by "faith alone" (v. 24). On the other hand, some have misunderstood James to mean that good works are needed in addition to faith, that is, apart from faith. James, however, never separates deeds from faith. He would agree with Paul, that Christians are saved by grace through faith, not through law-keeping (Romans 3:28). It is the implanted word humbly accepted through faith that saves (James 1:21). Deeds are no good unless they grow out of faith.

James does not discuss baptism in his letter, but his teaching on faith and deeds has implications for the doctrine of baptism. If believers separate any command, even the command to be baptized, from faith, they have made it a legalistic work that cannot save. Baptism does not follow faith as if they were separate, unrelated actions. Baptism shows faith. It is the natural outgrowth of faith. It is not a legal requirement but an act of faith.

2:19 You believe that there is one God. Good! Even the demons believe that — and shudder.

What is true of baptism is true of all Christian acts. Our deeds must show our faith. Merely to believe in God, even to fear him, is not enough. To make a verbal confession of faith is not enough. The basic biblical confession is that "God is one" (Deuteronomy 6:4; Matthew 19:17; Mark 12:29; 1 Corinthians 8:6; Ephesians 4:6; 1 Timothy 2:5). This confession, called the *Shema*, is still heard in synagogues today. It is also the heart of the Christian faith.

James says if you believe in one God, then so far, so good. However, if this is just a verbal faith it is not enough. Even the demons make this confession and shudder (φρίσσω, *phrissō*, "tremble with fear") in the presence of the Holy God and his Christ (Mark 1:23-24; 5:7; Acts 16:17, 19:15). Demons have faith. They believe the true orthodox doctrine that there is one God. Are they saved? Of course not! Why not? They do not put that faith into practice by caring for humans; instead they try to destroy them. One who is certain of his orthodoxy but refuses to help others has this same demonic faith.

James is not in tension with Paul when it comes to faith and works. He may, however, be fighting a misconception of Paul's teaching, a misunderstanding Paul himself confronts. Having painted a vibrant picture of salvation by grace through faith, Paul asks, "Shall we go on sinning that grace may increase?" (Romans 6:1). Some were taking Paul's teaching on grace and faith as a license for immorality (Romans 3:8). He reminds them that they died to sin in baptism and no longer live under its power (Romans 6:1-14).

James may be fighting the same misunderstanding, that as long as one has an inward "faith" then one is saved, no matter how one acts. But even the demons have such faith. They even recognize Jesus as God's Son, when others do not believe in him (Mark 1:24; 5:7; Luke 4:34). No one believes such demonic faith can save. James is not a legalist, but he speaks to those who have left legalism for an easy "faith" that does not even feed the hungry.

2:20 You foolish man, do you want evidence that faith without deeds is useless? 2:21 Was not our ancestor Abraham considered righteous for what he did when he offered his son Isaac on the altar?

To think that such faith without deeds can save is foolish. To illustrate, James gives two Old Testament examples. The first is Abraham, the father of the faithful and the great example of faith from the Old Testament. God promised a son to Abraham in his old age. "Abraham believed God, and it was credited to him as righteousness" (Genesis 15:6, quoted by James in v. 23).

However, Abraham's faith was not merely inward. He showed his faith by his actions, particularly by his sacrifice of Isaac. He did not actually kill Isaac; but by laying him bound on the altar and raising the knife, Abraham showed his willingness to obey God and so passed the test of faith. Although God had already credited Abraham's faith, it is when Abraham raised the knife that the angel of the Lord says, "Now I know that you fear God . . ." (Genesis 22:12).

2:22 You see that his faith and his actions were working together, and his faith was made complete by what he did. 2:23 And the scripture was fulfilled that says, "Abraham believed God, and it was credited to him as righteousness,"
The faith that counted for righteousness for Abraham was an active faith, not just a verbal one. His actions completed his faith, that is, they showed it was living, true faith. To James, the sacrifice of Isaac in Genesis 22 fulfills the prediction of Genesis 15:6 that Abraham's faith was credited (λογίζομαι, *logizomai*) to him as righteousness.

and he was called God's friend.
As a result of the faith he displayed, Abraham is called the "friend" (φίλος, *philos*) of God (cf. 2 Chronicles 20:7; Isaiah 41:8). No closer relationship to God can be imagined. Jesus uses this same language of "friends" for his disciples (John 15:13-15). Later James gives a clear choice to his readers. They can be either friends of the world or friends of God (James 4:4). Here Abraham becomes God's friend through the faith he put into action. If Christians are to be friends of God, they, like Abraham, must put faith into practice. One is reminded of Jesus' statement to those who claimed to be Abraham's children: "If you were Abraham's children, then

you would do the things Abraham did" (John 8:39).

2:24 You see that a person is justified by what he does and not by faith alone.

The conclusion James draws from the Abraham example is "that one is justified by what he does and not by faith alone." Paul uses Abraham to make a very different point, namely, that he was justified without works because his faith was credited to him as righteousness (Romans 4:1-5; Galatians 3:5-9). This raises several questions: Do Paul and James contradict each other? Is James correcting Paul, or is Paul correcting James? If they are not reacting to the other, why do they both use Abraham as an example?

First, it does appear that verbally Paul and James disagree. Paul says Abraham was justified by faith without works. James says he was justified by works, not by faith alone. On closer examination, the disagreement disappears. They use the words "works" and "faith" differently. By "works," Paul means the works of the Law, including the ceremony of circumcision. One is not saved by such works but by faith.

James would agree with this, but when he uses "works" he means not works of the Law but works that spring from faith. As we have seen above, to Paul, "faith" includes action. James uses "faith" in two ways: for faith that is merely claimed and therefore dead and for the true faith that shows itself in deeds. So was Abraham justified by faith or works? By faith, not by works of the Law. Yet not by a dead faith, but by a faith that showed itself in the act of sacrificing Isaac.

Paul and James are fighting different enemies. Paul fights the circumcision group who insists both Jews and Gentiles are saved by keeping the Law. James fights those nominal Christians who claim faith but do not practice it. This is why they use the Abraham example differently. But why do they both use that example? As we saw above, James may be correcting the misconception that Paul's view of faith demanded less obedience from Christians. If so, he may have intentionally chosen the Abraham example to show that Abraham was saved by an obedient faith.

However, it is quite possible that Paul and James are not reacting to each other at all, but that each independently chose to speak of Abraham. After all, Abraham is the prime example of faith in the Old Testament. In the Apocrypha, he is even an example of one found faithful for his deeds (1 Maccabees 2:51-52). The writer of Hebrews says Abraham offered up Isaac by faith (Hebrews 11:17). Thus, if one wants to speak of faith or deeds, Abraham springs to mind.

2:25 In the same way, was not even Rahab the prostitute considered righteous for what she did

Rahab, the second example of working faith, may seem at first to be an odd choice. Of all the Old Testament examples James could have chosen, why pick a Gentile and a prostitute? The answer may lie in the previous warning against favoritism. Christians are not to prefer rich to poor, so James gives both the rich and powerful Abraham and the despised prostitute Rahab as examples of faith. James's readers may have thought the example of Abraham's sacrifice of Isaac was too heroic for them to imitate. James says if one cannot be an Abraham, one can at least be a Rahab. Interestingly, the writer of Hebrews also gives both examples (Hebrews 11:31).

when she gave lodging to the spies and sent them off in a different direction?

Rahab hid the Israelite spies from their enemies in Jericho because she knew the Lord their God was the God of heaven and earth (Joshua 2:11). Unlike the demons and those who say "keep warm and well-fed," she confessed God and put that confession into practice by caring for God's people. Although they were strangers to her, she saved their lives for the sake of their God. Even though she was a stranger to the Law, as a result of her faithful actions, she and her household were saved from the destruction of Jericho and welcomed into Israel (Joshua 6:25). She is the embodiment of those who show mercy to others and so receive mercy from God.

2:26 As the body without the spirit is dead, so faith without deeds is dead.

James ends this section on faith and deeds by repeating that faith without action is dead (cf. 2:17). Such faith is like the body without the spirit, that is, without the life-giving force, the breath of life, that sustains it (cf. Genesis 6:17; 7:15; Psalm 104:29; Luke 23:46; John 19:30). This breath or spirit is not a mere addition to the body but the force that animates it. To separate faith from deeds is like separating the spirit from the body. It is death.

Section Summary and Application:

Again, James presents us with a clear choice. We can claim faith without works. We can look religious and even deceive ourselves into thinking we are people of faith while we neglect the needs of our brothers and sisters. Such a "faith" is really no faith at all. It does not help the needy. It cannot save. It is the faith of the demons. It is dead. Faith shown by deeds is the faith that saves, the faith of Abraham and Rahab. Like them, we must trust and obey.

JAMES 3

IX. TAMING THE TONGUE (3:1-12)

¹Not many of you should presume to be teachers, my brothers, because you know that we who teach will be judged more strictly. ²We all stumble in many ways. If anyone is never at fault in what he says, he is a perfect man, able to keep his whole body in check.

³When we put bits into the mouths of horses to make them obey us, we can turn the whole animal. ⁴Or take ships as an example. Although they are so large and are driven by strong winds, they are steered by a very small rudder wherever the pilot wants to go. ⁵Likewise the tongue is a small part of the body, but it makes great boasts. Consider what a great forest is set on fire by a small spark. ⁶The tongue also is a fire, a world of evil among the parts of the body. It corrupts the whole person, sets the whole course of his life on fire, and is itself set on fire by hell.

⁷All kinds of animals, birds, reptiles and creatures of the sea are being tamed and have been tamed by man, ⁸but no man can tame the tongue. It is a restless evil, full of deadly poison.

⁹With the tongue we praise our Lord and Father, and with it we curse men, who have been made in God's likeness. ¹⁰Out of the same mouth come praise and cursing. My brothers, this should not be. ¹¹Can both fresh water and salt[a] water flow from the same spring? ¹²My brothers, can a fig tree bear olives, or a grapevine bear figs? Neither can a salt spring produce fresh water.

[a]*11* Greek *bitter* (see also verse 14)

In 1:19 James says one should be slow to speak and in 1:26 he states that one cannot have true religion without reining in the tongue. In this section he returns to that theme. As with his other strong words of exhortation, James softens the blow by addressing his readers warmly as "brothers" three times in this section (3:1,10,12).

3:1 Not many of you should presume to be teachers, my brothers,

He begins with a curt instruction: "Not many of you become teachers." The teacher or rabbi was an honored position in ancient Judaism and early Christianity. Jesus himself was often called "Teacher" (διδασκολος, *didaskolos*) by the scribes as well as by his disciples (Matthew 8:19; 23:8-10; Mark 4:38; Luke 9:38; John 13:13-14). Certain leaders in the early church were also called teachers (Acts 13:1; 1 Corinthians 12:28-29; Romans 12:7; Ephesians 4:11; 1 Timothy 2:7; 2 Timothy 1:11). The role of teacher overlapped with other types of leaders in the early church such as preachers, missionaries, elders, and apostles. It is, therefore, hard to define precisely the office of teacher, but it was a position of influence.

Because of the prominence given to teachers, one might be tempted to aspire to the position out of a desire for recognition instead of a calling to serve. Jesus condemns those who love to be seen by others and greeted as "Rabbi" (Matthew 23:5-7). It is difficult, even today, for teachers or ministers to keep a proper humility when hundreds or even thousands of people are hanging on their every word. The temptation for teachers to say what people want to hear in order to be popular is also not a new one (2 Timothy 4:3; compare Paul's insistence that he had not hesitated to proclaim the whole will of God to the Ephesians, Acts 20:27). The NIV thus translates, "Not many of you should presume to be teachers."

because you know that we who teach will be judged more strictly.

The teacher's role in the church is not to be taken hastily

for it carries with it a peculiar danger; the teacher uses the unruly tongue. While all Christians can sin with the tongue, teachers are particularly vulnerable for several reasons. First, they simply have more opportunities for speaking. Teachers by definition must speak and not be silent; because they use many words, they are more likely to be at fault in their speech.

Second, teachers are often tempted to use their pulpits or classrooms to boast of their own knowledge and speak derisively of those who disagree with them. Discussion of positions and issues easily degenerates into character assassination. Teachers may have the desire to set people straight or even to tell them off. It is right for scholars to be hard on ideas but easy on people. Unfortunately, the opposite often is the case. There are still those who "preach Christ out of selfish ambition, not sincerely, supposing they can stir up trouble . . ." (Philippians 1:17).

What teachers say can do damage to others, even if they speak with kindness. There is such a thing as false teaching that can cost listeners their salvation if they follow it (cf. Matthew 5:19; 18:6). Sincerity in itself is no guarantee that what a teacher says is healthy teaching. Teachers must be certain they are teaching the truth and not deceiving themselves and their students. Even if they believe the truth themselves, teachers must be careful to communicate it clearly and not inadvertently to lead others astray. Lack of serious preparation for teaching can result in as much harm as intentionally spreading false doctrine. The teacher is always in danger of falling in love with his own voice, claiming knowledge he does not have and so turning to "meaningless talk" (1 Timothy 1:6).

Finally, a teacher of the Bible cannot easily claim ignorance of God's commands. The one who knows more has a greater responsibility to serve as a moral example. To do otherwise is hypocrisy (cf. Romans 2:17-24) Although no teacher is perfect, "Do what I say, not what I do" will not convince many of the truth. As Jesus said, "That servant who knows his master's will and does not get ready or does not do what his master wants will be beaten with many blows. But the one who does not know and does things deserving punishment will be beaten with few blows. From everyone who has been given much, much will be demanded; and from the one who has been entrusted with much, much more will be asked" (Luke 12:47-48).

James also says teachers (including himself by using "we") "will be judged more strictly." This may mean that a higher standard (literally, "a greater judgment") will be applied to them. Everyone will be responsible on the day of judgment for every careless word spoken (Matthew 12:36). Since teachers have more opportunity for careless words, their responsibility will be greater on that day.

The words "will be judged more strictly" can also be translated "will be punished more severely." The idea of degrees of punishment in the afterlife may be strange to some but is supported by the "many blows, few blows" passage above and by other sayings of Jesus (Matthew 23:13 in some manuscripts; Luke 20:47). In most of these passages, the stricter punishment is specifically directed against the teachers of the law. It is likely then, that James also threatens teachers with more severe punishment. This verse is not an invitation to speculate on the exact shape of the afterlife but rather the strongest warning possible against hastily becoming a teacher.

3:2 We all stumble in many ways. If anyone is never at fault in what he says, he is a perfect man, able to keep his whole body in check.

The high calling of teacher does not demand sinless perfection, for "we all stumble in many ways" (cf. James 2:10; Romans 3:23; 1 John 1:8). It does demand that one strive to control the tongue. If one could avoid all mistakes in speech, then he would be perfect (τέλειος, *teleios*, perfection here understood as maturity as in James 1:4; cf. Matthew 5:48). This seems at first like a strange statement from James. After all, he has said repeatedly that religious speech is not enough; action is required (2:12,14,16,18).

To James, however, controlling speech is itself an act of faith. If one can control the tongue, then one can control the body. This self-control is necessary for true ethical action. Just as there should be no separation between faith and deeds, so also there should be no separation between speech and life. Teachers should both practice what they preach and preach what they practice. This requires controlling the tongue.

3:3 When we put bits into the mouths of horses to make them obey us, we can turn the whole animal.

Although he does not leave his concern for teachers behind, verses 2-12 have application to all the brothers. Not just teachers, but all must fight to control the tongue. James shows the difficulty of that task by illustrating the power of the tongue with examples of large objects controlled by very small parts. In 1:26 James spoke of "keeping a tight rein" on the tongue. Here, in verse 2b, using a different form of the Greek word, he returns to the image of the bit and the horse: "he is able to rein in his whole body" (NIV, "keep his whole body in check"). A large horse is turned by a small bit in its mouth. This was a common illustration in the ancient world, used by Plato and Sophocles in other contexts. In the same way, a human being also can control his whole body by controlling his mouth (v. 2). Not just control, but restraint is pictured by the horse's bit. We must say "whoa" to our words before we speak them too hastily.

3:4 Or take ships as an example. Although they are so large and are driven by strong winds, they are steered by a very small rudder wherever the pilot wants to go.

The second example, a ship controlled by a rudder, was also well-known, having been used by Aristotle and others. The difference between the large object and the small controller is even greater here. The largest ship is turned by a relatively tiny rudder under the control of a pilot. Strong winds are mentioned to show the danger of misusing a rudder. One small slip can sink the ship. One small slip of the tongue can also destroy lives. As the rider's will controls the horse through the small bit in its mouth, so the pilot's will controls the huge ship through a small rudder.

3:5 Likewise the tongue is a small part of the body, but it makes great boasts.

Yet the human will cannot control the tongue. Instead, the small tongue makes great boasts (αὐχέω, *aucheō*) and controls one's entire life. "Boasting" may be a reference to those who hastily proclaim themselves teachers and brag of their intellectual and spiritual attainments.

Consider what a great forest is set on fire by a small spark. 3:6 The tongue also is a fire,

The most lengthy illustration is that the tongue is like a fire. This illustration begins with another large-small contrast, a large forest can be destroyed by the smallest of sparks. There is a play on words here, since the same Greek word (ἡλίκος, *hēlikos*, which points to size in either direction) is used for the largeness of the forest and the smallness of the spark. Words that seem small and insignificant can spread rapidly like wildfire, destroying countless relationships (cf. Proverbs 16:27; 26:20-21). No wonder James extends this illustration by saying that the tongue is not simply *like* a fire, but it *is* a fire.

a world of evil among the parts of the body.

The next phrase in Greek is difficult to translate,[1] but the NIV reading is a good one: "a world of evil among the parts of the body." The use of "world" (κόσμος, *kosmos*) reflects the command "to keep oneself from being polluted by the world" (James 1:27) and anticipates the discussion of friendship of the world in 4:4. The world is any aspect of human culture that keeps one from God. "World" also implies the vast extent of the damage done by the tongue.

---

[1] There are five nominative words or phrases here in Greek, so the difficulty is deciding how they are related to one another.

Some have suggested that "the whole body" (NIV, "the whole person") here refers to the church; thus James is warning against teachers who lead the church astray and so corrupt the body of Christ. This seems unlikely. James instead is talking about controlling the self by controlling the tongue, as in v. 2.

It corrupts the whole person, sets the whole course of his life on fire,

Failure to control the tongue will corrupt (or "pollute," σπιλόω, *spiloō*) the "whole person" (as the NIV translates). This is the opposite of the pure and faultless religion that keeps one unpolluted by the world (James 1:27).

"The course (or circle) of life" was a significant phrase in Orphic religion, a type of paganism begun several centuries before Christ. Originally it expressed the doctrine of eternal recurrence, that humans are at the mercy of the turns of the wheel of fate, and what has been will be again. By the time James writes, it had lost most of its religious flavor and simply meant the changing fortunes of life. The point is that the fire of the tongue affects every aspect of life.

and is itself set on fire by hell.

James locates the origin of the fire of the tongue in hell itself. Significantly, this is the only time the word "hell" (γέεννα, *gehenna*) is used outside of the Gospels.[2] *Gehenna* is literally the Valley of Hinnom near Jerusalem where pagan sacrifices were offered in the Old Testament (Joshua 15:8; 18:16; 2 Kings 16:3; 21:6; 23:10). Jeremiah calls it "the Valley of Slaughter" (Jeremiah 7:32; 19:6) because of God's judgment against paganism. By the intertestamental period, the valley had become a symbol of the punishment of the last judgment.

James's use of *gehenna* reflects the sayings of Jesus, particularly in the Sermon on the Mount. Jesus connects speech

---

[2]See Hans Scharen, "Gehenna in the Synoptics," *Bibiotheca Sacra* 149 (October-December 1992), 454-470, for more on the use of the word in the Gospels and James.

(saying "You Fool!") to punishment in hell (Matthew 5:22). He warns that it is better to lose one part of the body, an eye or a hand, than for the whole body to be thrown into hell (Matthew 5:29-30). James uses the same Greek word (μέλος, *melos*, "part of the body") for the tongue (v. 5). Just as an eye or hand can lead one to hell, according to Jesus, so the tongue is a fire from hell, according to James.

Since James began this section on the tongue with a warning to teachers, he might also be influenced by Jesus' words to the teachers of the Law that they convert someone only "to make him twice a son of hell as you are" (Matthew 23:15). Jesus implies their teaching is from hell, and they are headed there. James warns teachers of stricter punishment and states the tongue has its origin in hell. Since Satan is associated with hell, this is another way of saying that the evil of the tongue is not just the result of human desire (as in James 1:14-15) but of Satan's influence.

3:7 All kinds of animals, birds, reptiles and creatures of the sea are being tamed and have been tamed by man,

Since the evil power of the tongue is from hell or Satan, the tongue is not completely natural. God gave Adam (Genesis 1:26-28) and later Noah (Genesis 9:2) power over nature, that is, over the animals God created. The four classes of creatures here are the same as in Genesis 9:2; they stand for the entire animal kingdom (cf. Deuteronomy 4:17-18; 1 Kings 4:33). God has given humans the ability to tame all kinds of these creatures (cf. Psalm 8:6-8), yet even the wildest beast is easier to control than one's own tongue. The lion tamer in the center ring of the circus is in less danger than anyone who has a tongue.

3:8 but no man can tame the tongue. It is a restless evil, full of deadly poison.

The only other time the word "tame" (δαμάζω, *damazō*) is used in the New Testament is in the story of the demon-possessed man whom no one was strong enough to tame (Mark

5:4). In the same way, one cannot tame the tongue because its evil was not made by God. It is not God's creation but Satan's. This is hyperbole. James is not saying the physical tongue was not made by God, but rather, if left unrestrained, the evil of the tongue becomes even demonic. To use an Old Testament example, the tongue is like the poison of a snake (Psalms 58:3-4; 140:3; cf. Romans 3:13).

The tongue can be used for good; one can even use it to praise God. The problem is that the tongue is not consistently good. One of the greatest evils of the tongue is inconsistency. James calls it "a restless evil." The Greek word translated "restless" (ἀκατάστατος, *akatastatos*) is used in James 1:8 to describe the double-minded man as "unstable." Just as the doubter in chapter one is unsure in his prayers to God, so the tongue is inconsistent in praise.

3:9 With the tongue we praise our Lord and Father, and with it we curse men, who have been made in God's likeness.

By using "we" James includes himself as one prone to inconsistency: we praise "our Lord and Father" (a phrase found only here in the Bible) and curse people with the same tongue. This is equivalent to both praising and cursing God, since humans bear God's image or likeness (Genesis 1:26-28). "Praise" (εὐλογέω, *eulogeō*) is literally "to bless." "Blessed be the Lord" is the typical Old Testament phrase for praise. The phrase was also used by the early church (Romans 1:25; 9:5; 2 Corinthians 1:3; 11:31; Ephesians 1:3; 1 Peter 1:3).[3]

3:10 Out of the same mouth come praise and cursing. My brothers, this should not be.

Cursing here does not refer to the biblical practice of calling on God to punish others, as the Psalmist frequently does or like Paul handing over certain ones to Satan (1 Corinthians

---

[3]See Christopher Wright Mitchell, *The Meaning of BRK "To Bless" in the Old Testament* (Atlanta: Scholars Press, 1987).

5:5; 1 Timothy 1:20). Paul can even say, "If anyone does not love the Lord — a curse be on him" (1 Corinthians 16:22). Rather, James has in mind the personal curse that displays hatred toward the brother, as in Jesus' warning that calling a brother "fool" is as punishable as murder (Matthew 5:21-22).[4]

The Bible affirms that one who claims to love and serve God while hating a fellow human is a liar (1 John 4:19). Few Christians would admit hatred for others, but their speech betrays them. They sing God's praises loud in church on Sunday then wound others, even those closest to them, with their words the rest of the week. Such inconsistency is unthinkable to James: "My brothers, this should not be."

3:11 Can both fresh water and salt water flow from the same spring? 3:12 My brothers, can a fig tree bear olives, or a grapevine bear figs? Neither can a salt spring produce fresh water.

Inconsistency is also unnatural. Sweet and bitter waters do not come from the same source. This is an interesting example in light of Israel's experience in the wilderness. At Marah, it took a miracle from God to turn bitter water to sweet (Exodus 15:23-25). God's power is also needed to make our speech consistent. Plants produce only after their kind (cf. Matthew 7:16-17). God made nature to be consistent. The tongue is inconsistent. It does not keep to its proper place in the creation but partakes of another, evil nature, that of hell itself.

Section Summary and Application:

James's portrait of the evils of the tongue seems relentlessly gloomy. Teachers in particular are subject to the dangers of the tongue, but they are not alone. The small tongue controls the whole person. It is a fire from hell. Unlike nature, it is inconsistent. It cannot be tamed.

---

[4]For more on blessing and cursing, see Mary J. Evans, "'A Plague on Both Your Houses': Cursing and Blessing Reviewed," *Vox Evangelica* 24 (1994), 77-89.

If all this is true, why should we even try to control the tongue? It seems a hopeless cause. Yet James expects us to make every effort to be slow to speak (1:19), to rein in the tongue (1:26), and to avoid slander (4:11). How is this possible? The answer is found in a brief phrase in 3:8, "No man can tame the tongue." No man can, but God can. If the tongue is set on fire of hell, there is One who is greater than hell, One who has triumphed over Satan. James later will urge submission to God (4:7). God alone has the power to subdue the unruly tongue if we will only trust in him.

What is at stake here is not just watching our words but being controlled by God. "For out of the overflow of the heart the mouth speaks" (Matthew 12:34b). James is not pointing so much to self-improvement but to character. Whether or not we are teachers, the real question is, "Who controls our speech?" or rather, "Who controls our life?" James reminds us that the true answer to this question is not seen in our intentions but in our speech and actions.

X. WISDOM, EARTHLY AND HEAVENLY (3:13-18)

¹³Who is wise and understanding among you? Let him show it by his good life, by deeds done in the humility that comes from wisdom. ¹⁴But if you harbor bitter envy and selfish ambition in your hearts, do not boast about it or deny the truth. ¹⁵Such "wisdom" does not come down from heaven but is earthly, unspiritual, of the devil. ¹⁶For where you have envy and selfish ambition, there you find disorder and every evil practice.

¹⁷But the wisdom that comes from heaven is first of all pure; then peace-loving, considerate, submissive, full of mercy and good fruit, impartial and sincere. ¹⁸Peacemakers who sow in peace raise a harvest of righteousness.

James returns to the theme of wisdom, first found in 1:5-8. See the comments there on the nature of wisdom and its Old

Testament background. Wisdom is also a virtue in the New Testament (Matthew 23:34; Romans 16:19; 1 Corinthians 6:5; Ephesians 5:15). Some suggest that James is still directing his words at the teachers whom he warned in 3:1. Teachers claimed wisdom and might be tempted toward envy and ambition, which James condemns below. While this focus on teachers is possible, this is, more likely, a general admonition from James to all his readers. They should follow true wisdom, not the "wisdom" of the age.

3:13 Who is wise and understanding among you?

James begins this section with a question, characteristic of the diatribe form he likes so well: "Who is wise and understanding among you?" Wisdom is linked with understanding (ἐπιστήμων, *epistēmōn*, a word found only here in the Greek New Testament). "Understanding" is a synonym for "wisdom" (σοφία, *sophia*) that emphasizes the intellectual aspect of knowledge. The two words were so frequently linked in the Old Testament (Deuteronomy 1:13; 4:6; 1 Kings 4:29; Job 28:28; Daniel 1:4) that they had become a single term: "wise and understanding."

Let him show it by his good life, by deeds done in the humility that comes from wisdom.

If one is truly wise, he will show it by his conduct, just as one shows faith by deeds (James 2:18). A merely verbal claim to wisdom is no better than a verbal claim to faith. Biblical wisdom is never intellectual attainment alone; it is a way of living in harmony with God and others. Jesus said, "Wisdom is proved right by her actions" (Matthew 11:19).

The actions of true wisdom display humility or meekness. Ancient Greek moralists thought meekness was a virtue that could easily become a weakness, making one a victim. In the New Testament, however, the word is always positive. Jesus blesses the meek (Matthew 5:5) and describes himself as meek (Matthew 11:29). Christians are exhorted to follow his example (1 Corinthians 4:21; 2 Corinthians 10:1; Galatians 5:23;

6:1; Ephesians 4:2; Colossians 3:12; 2 Timothy 2:25; Titus 3:2; 1 Peter 3:15).

In regard to people, meekness includes a warm and gentle friendliness that James earlier contrasted with anger (1:20-21). As describing one's relation to God, it implies a humble acceptance of his will. Thus, the word that saves must be humbly accepted (1:21). One who is truly wise will not boast of his knowledge and insight, as if he had gained wisdom by his own power. Instead, true wisdom is the gift of the one who gives generously (James 1:5). Christians must receive that gift with gratitude and humility.

3:14 But if you harbor bitter envy and selfish ambition in your hearts,

James contrasts this true, meek wisdom that comes from God with a so-called "wisdom" that is worldly, focused solely on this life. The argument here is similar to his argument on the two types of faith (2:14-26). Faith without deeds is dead. It is no faith at all. So a wisdom that is not humble is really no wisdom at all. Such a wisdom springs not from humility before God and meekness before neighbor but from bitter envy and selfish ambition.

The word translated "envy" (ζῆλος, *zelos*) is sometimes used positively in the New Testament for enthusiastic commitment: "zeal" (John 2:17; Romans 10:2; 2 Corinthians 7:11; 9:2; Philippians 3:6). Many times the term is used for those who are enthusiastically committed to their own advancement at the expense of others: "envy" or "jealousy" (Acts 5:17; 13:45; Romans 13:13; 1 Corinthians 3:3; 2 Corinthians 12:20; Galatians 5:20). Sometimes even zeal for God can be perverted into personal rivalry with others. James calls this envy "bitter," (πικρός, *pikros*), the same word he used to describe the salt or bitter water in v. 11. Envy embitters and poisons relationships. Like bitter water, it promises life but brings death.

Coupled with envy is selfish ambition (ἐριθεία, *eritheia*). This word is used by Aristotle to refer to partisan political fights. Here it points to the attitude of unrestrained self-promotion that gathers a group of admirers around oneself and so leads to division in the church (cf. Romans 2:8; 1 Corinthians 1:11-12; 2 Corinthians 12:20; Galatians 5:20; Philippians 1:17). "Ambition" is a positive word to most contemporary people. James reminds his readers that one realizes personal ambition often at the expense of others.

do not boast about it or deny the truth.

Bitter envy and selfish ambition find their home in the heart, the seat of emotion, purpose, and character (Genesis 6:5; Exodus 4:21; Deuteronomy 6:6; Psalm 11:2; cf. James 1:26; 4:8). Such inner attitudes cannot be hidden for long. Soon they show themselves in boasting (see v. 5) and in denying the truth (literally, "lie against the truth"). The last phrase may be a redundant phrase, or may be a reference to opposing the word of truth that gives new birth (James 1:18).

3:15 Such "wisdom" does not come down from heaven

There is "wisdom" or common sense in ambition and self-promotion. "Looking out for number one" seems to work well in the world. Such wisdom, however, does not come down from heaven (in Greek, "from above"). It is not one of the good and perfect gifts of the Father above (James 1:17). Instead, it progresses (or rather, digresses) from earthly to unspiritual to demonic.

but is earthly, unspiritual, of the devil.

"Earthly" (ἐπίγειος, *epigeios*) means this so-called wisdom is merely human, not from God above (cf. John 3:12; 1 Corinthians 15:40; 2 Corinthians 5:1; Philippians 3:19). This description is similar to Paul's discussion of "the wisdom of the world" in 1 Corinthians 1:18-2:5.

This "wisdom" is also unspiritual. In Greek (ψυχικός, *psychikos*), it is literally "of the soul." It is a wisdom of the natural person (cf. 1 Corinthians 15:44,46), not the spiritual person. Ambitious, envious wisdom is not from the Holy Spirit. To one who has such "wisdom," the words and ways of the Spirit seem foolish (1 Corinthians 2:13-14). Such men "follow mere natural instincts and do not have the Spirit" (Jude 19).

Finally, such wisdom is demonic. It is not just a lower form of wisdom but is in direct opposition to God. As the tongue is set on fire by hell (James 3:6), so this wisdom has its source in the realm of Satan. Demons have a type of faith (James 2:19); they also have a type of wisdom. However, Christians should avoid such wisdom at all costs since they are to have nothing to do with the works of demons (1 Corinthians 10:20-21; 1 Timothy 4:1).

3:16 For where you have envy and selfish ambition, there you find disorder and every evil practice.

Envy and selfish ambition lead to disorder. This is a different form of the word used to describe the "unstable" double-minded man (James 1:8) and the "restless" evil of the tongue (James 3:8). Envy and ambition cause instability and restlessness in human relationships. They can split and completely destroy a church (2 Corinthians 12:20), resulting in every kind of mean and underhanded practice. As Thomas Campbell said, "That division among the Christians is a horrid evil, fraught with many evils."[5]

3:17 But the wisdom that comes from heaven

James contrasts this worldly wisdom with the wisdom from above by giving a list of virtues that come from heavenly wisdom. Such virtue lists were common among Greek moralists and are found elsewhere in the New Testament. This list is quite similar to a description of wisdom in the Apocrypha (Wisdom of Solomon 7:22-30). It also resembles the Beatitudes (Matthew 5:3-12) and the fruit of the Spirit (Galatians 5:22-23). Indeed, in James, wisdom functions as the Holy Spirit does in the rest of the New Testament. It is the

---

[5]Thomas Campbell, *The Declaration and Address*, in Charles Alexander Young, ed., *Historical Documents Advocating Christian Union* (Joplin, MO: College Press, 1985), p. 112.

gift of God (James 1:5) that produces fruit, the "harvest of righteousness" (James 3:18).[6]

is first of all pure;

Wisdom calls for purity. Pure implies moral and spiritual virtue as well as singleness of will. The double-minded person cannot receive wisdom from God because he lacks that purity of will (James 1:6-8). Later, James will exhort the double-minded to purify their hearts (James 4:8). Since the character of God is described as pure (1 John 3:3), then only those pure in heart will see him (Matthew 5:8).

then peace-loving, considerate, submissive, full of mercy and good fruit, impartial and sincere.

True wisdom works for peace (cf. Matthew 5:9; Galatians 5:22; Romans 12:18; Ephesians 6:15; Hebrews 12:11,14). The biblical idea of peace is more than the absence of war or conflict. It describes harmonious relations within an individual and between members of a society. In Hebrew, peace (*shalom*) is used as a greeting and also as a way of inquiring after someone's state of being. To be at peace is to be happy, to be whole, to be right with God, fellow humans, and creation. Peace is the opposite of the rivalry, instability, and division brought by envy and ambition.

Wisdom is also considerate and submissive (cf. 2 Corinthians 10:1; Philippians 4:5; 1 Timothy 3:3; Titus 3:2). These two words both point to an attitude that thinks of others instead of self. True wisdom does not insist on its own way but is open to persuasion from others. The wise person is compliant and reasonable, not a know-it-all. He "listens carefully to the other instead of attacking him."[7]

Wisdom is shown by actions, good fruit, that stem from mercy (cf. Matthew 5:7). As true religion cares for widows and

---

[6]See J.A. Kirk, "The Meaning of Wisdom in James: Examination of a Hypothesis," *New Testament Studies* 16 (1969), 24-38.

[7]Peter Davids, *The Epistle of James*. New International Greek Testament, (Grand Rapids: Eerdmans, 1982), p. 154.

orphans (James 1:27), and true faith clothes the naked and feeds the hungry (James 2:15-17), so true wisdom produces acts of mercy and compassion for those in need.

Wisdom is impartial. This may mean the wise avoid favoritism. They do not prefer certain persons over others on the basis of their appearance or position (James 2:1-11). However, this Greek word (ἀδιάκριτος, *adiakritos*) for impartial can also be translated, "unwavering." Wisdom does not have the restless inconsistency of the evil tongue (James 3:9-12) but is wholehearted in its devotion to God.

Finally wisdom is sincere (ἀνυπόκριτος, *anypokritos*, cf. Romans 12:9; 2 Corinthians 6:6; 1 Timothy 1:5; 2 Timothy 1:5). True wisdom does not have to show off. It does not have the pretentious display of the ambitious. Jesus constantly denounced the hypocrisy of those who claimed to be wise but did not obey God (Matthew 6:2, 5, 16; 7:5; 15:7; Mark 12:15; Luke 12:56; 13:15). The truly wise are not hypocritical. They have a consistency between what they say and how they live.

3:18 Peacemakers who sow in peace raise a harvest of righteousness.

James ends his list with what sounds like a proverb: the one who sows peace reaps righteousness (for similar phrases, see Proverbs 11:30; Isaiah 32:16-17; Amos 6:12; 2 Corinthians 9:10; Galatians 5:22; Philippians 1:11; Hebrews 12:11). The repetition of different forms of "peace" shows that this is the central characteristic of wisdom to James. Wisdom from above always strives for harmony. Worldly wisdom, marked by envy and ambition, always disrupts relationships.

Section Summary and Application:

This section on two types of wisdom has great relevance for Christians today. What passes for wisdom or common sense in our world is shaped by the entertainment media, self-help books, and success seminars. This "wisdom" tells us that positive thinking, self-promotion, and tapping into hidden internal resources will bring happiness, excellence, and success. Such thinking is not just "out there" in the world; it is taken for granted in the church. Like the original readers of James, we "have not traded in worldly views of power and importance for God's viewpoint."[8]

James talks of another type of wisdom, a heavenly common sense that is in direct opposition to the thinking of our age. This wisdom seeks peace, not success. It desires purity, not happiness. It shows itself in a willingness to yield to others, a sharp contrast to ambitious self-promotion.

Great courage is called for to reject worldly wisdom. To question the value of ambition and self-promotion marks one as strange and perhaps even irrational in the minds of most people. Some may call Christians lazy, critical, or even subversive to American ideals. Still, we must stand against this earthly, unspiritual, demonic "wisdom."

But how in the world can we achieve true wisdom if it is so foreign to natural common sense? James reminds us that such wisdom is not the result of human effort. It is from above, a gift of God that comes only through faithful prayer (James 1:5-8).

---

[8]Pheme Perkins, *First and Second Peter, James, and Jude,* Interpretation Commentary (Louisville: John Knox Press, 1995), p. 121.

JAMES 4

XI. FRIENDS OF THE WORLD OR OF GOD (4:1-10)

¹What causes fights and quarrels among you? Don't they come from your desires that battle within you? ²You want something but don't get it. You kill and covet, but you cannot have what you want. You quarrel and fight. You do not have, because you do not ask God. ³When you ask, you do not receive, because you ask with wrong motives, that you may spend what you get on your pleasures.

⁴You adulterous people, don't you know that friendship with the world is hatred toward God? Anyone who chooses to be a friend of the world becomes an enemy of God. ⁵Or do you think Scripture says without reason that the spirit he caused to live in us envies intensely?ᵃ ⁶But he gives us more grace. That is why Scripture says:

"God opposes the proud but gives grace to the humble."ᵇ

⁷Submit yourselves, then, to God. Resist the devil, and he will flee from you. ⁸Come near to God and he will come near to you. Wash your hands, you sinners, and purify your hearts, you double-minded. ⁹Grieve, mourn and wail. Change your laughter to mourning and your joy to gloom. ¹⁰Humble yourselves before the Lord, and he will lift you up.

ᵃ5 Or *that God jealously longs for the spirit that he made to live in us; or that the Spirit he causes to live in us longs jealously*   ᵇ6 Prov. 3:34

4:1 What causes fights and quarrels among you?

In the tradition of the Old Testament prophets, James denounces in this section those who turn from God to the world. As is his style (cf. James 2:4, 5, 6, 7, 14, 16, 20, 21, 25;

3:11, 12, 13), he begins with a leading question: "What causes fights and quarrels among you?" These are military terms: "wars" (πόλεμοι, *polemoi*) and "battles" (μάχαι, *machai*). James means them figuratively; his readers were not having pitched battles but were fighting and quarreling (cf. 2 Corinthians 7:5; 2 Timothy 2:23; Titus 3:9) Even today, church fights can be bitter and hateful. Such "wars" come from the envy of worldly wisdom and are a startling contrast to the peace brought by true wisdom that James just discussed (James 3:17-18).

Don't they come from your desires that battle within you?

What is the source of conflict among Christians? James says these external fights are the result of an internal battle. They come from the desire for personal pleasure (ἡδονή, *hēdonē*). This word, from which we get "hedonism," implies not the simple enjoyment of life but a mad dash for immediate pleasure that enslaves and separates one from God (cf. Luke 8:14; Titus 3:3; 2 Peter 2:13).

Earlier, James said that desires (ἐπιθυμία, *epithymia*, used as a verb in verse 2) lead to sin and to death (James 1:14-15). Here, these desires for pleasure battle, literally, "in your members" or the parts of their bodies (cf. James 3:6). This does not mean that physical pleasures are bad in themselves, but that they easily distract from God. Here, "members" of the body functions much like "the flesh" does in the writings of Paul, standing for that nature in humans that is opposed to God (Romans 7:23; Galatians 5:19-21). Worldly pleasures are not natural, not from God's good creation, but are acquired tastes that war against the best in his creatures.

4:2 You want something but don't get it. You kill and covet, but you cannot have what you want. You quarrel and fight.

Verse two should be punctuated differently than it is in the NIV: "You want something and do not get it, so you kill. You covet but cannot have what you want, so you quarrel and fight." The first sentence is quite shocking. Were James's readers allowing their desires to lead to actual murder?

Erasmus, the Renaissance scholar, tried to avoid the harshness of this phrase by suggesting it originally read "so you are jealous" (φθονεῖτε, *phthoneite*) instead of "so you murder" (φονεύετε, *phoneuete*). However, there is no evidence for this reading in any Greek manuscript.

Can frustrated desire lead to murder? It did with Cain and Abel (Genesis 4:2-8), with David and Uriah (2 Samuel 11), and with Ahab and Naboth (1 Kings 21). Fighting and killing are the logical outcome of envy. If someone stands in the way of one's desires, it makes sense to eliminate the competition. Jesus himself was delivered to death because of jealousy (Matthew 27:18). The apostles, Paul particularly, were often persecuted because their opponents were jealous (Acts 5:17; 13:45; 17:5). James's readers probably had not committed real murder because of their desire for pleasure, but they may have slandered and hated their brothers and sisters, which is the same as murder (Matthew 5:21-22; 1 John 3:12-15). James may also have in mind the neglect for the hungry brother or sister that could result in a literal death (James 2:16-17).

You do not have, because you do not ask God.

The great irony is that these Christians serve a God who generously gives all good and perfect gifts (James 1:17; cf. Matthew 7:7-8). He wants to give them true pleasure, but they refuse to ask. Instead, they prefer to seek their desires at the expense of others.

4:3 When you ask, you do not receive, because you ask with wrong motives, that you may spend what you get on your pleasures.

When they do ask God, they ask with wrong motives. Like the Prodigal Son, they spend their Father's gifts only on themselves (Luke 15:14). They "think that godliness is a means to financial gain" (1 Timothy 6:5b). Such prayers are the opposite of asking for daily bread (Matthew 6:11) and seeking God's kingdom first (Matthew 6:33). James will later say that prayer is powerful and effective but only for the righteous, that is, for those who seek God's will instead of their own pleasure (James 5:16).

To use God to obtain what one wants is an idolatrous form of prayer. It is the prayer of a pagan who believes the magic word will force the gods to do his bidding. Jesus warned against praying to God in this manner, since "your Father knows what you need before you ask him" (Matthew 6:8). Christians can pray for what they want but only as God wills. Prayer is not magical or mechanical. The children of God must have a personal relationship to the Father they address in prayer. When one prays for what brings pleasure without regard for the desires of others or for the will of God, he asks wrongly and should not expect an answer. God will not be manipulated by such prayers. To attempt to do so makes one unfaithful to him.

4:4 You adulterous people, don't you know that friendship with the world is hatred toward God? Anyone who chooses to be a friend of the world becomes an enemy of God.

Such unfaithfulness is like adultery. James literally calls them "adulteresses." The feminine form here (μοιχαλίδες, *moichalides*) has caused embarrassment to many scholars. Most translations (including the NIV) change it to include adulterers. However, the feminine is significant. James is reflecting the common Old Testament metaphor of Israel as the bride of the Lord (Isaiah 54:5-8; Jeremiah 2:1-2).[1] The prophets often condemn Israel as an adulteress for her unfaithfulness with other gods (Isaiah 57:3-9; Jeremiah 3:6-10, 20; 13:27; Ezekiel 16:32-42; Hosea 3:1; 9:1).

In the New Testament, the church is called the bride of Christ (2 Corinthians 11:2; Ephesians 5:22-33; Revelation

---

[1]John J. Schmidt, "You Adulteresses! The Image in James 4:4" *Novum Testamentum* 28 (1986), 327-337, does not believe James is referring to Israel as the bride of the Lord. Instead, he thinks this is a reference to Proverbs 30:20, "This is the way of an adulteress: She eats and wipes her mouth and says, 'I've done nothing wrong.'" James' readers have the same lack of remorse, he argues.

19:7-9; 21:2, 9). James extends the metaphor from the church as a whole to the individual Christian. Each Christian is to God as a wife to a husband. Thus, these Christians, like Israel of old, have broken their vows of exclusive allegiance to God to follow pleasure, one of the gods of their age and ours. They have become unfaithful to Christ, much like his own generation whom he called "adulterous" because of their lack of faith (Matthew 12:39; 16:4; Mark 8:38). Earlier James had summarized the law by mentioning two commandments: "Do not commit adultery" and "Do not murder" (James 2:11). Now (in vv. 1 and 4) he accuses his readers of both murder and adultery.

Like Paul (see Romans 6:16; 11:2; 1 Corinthians 3:16; 5:6; 6:2; 9:13), James confronts his readers by asking, "Do you not know?" They cannot be ignorant of the truth that friendship with the world is hatred toward God. Friendship was a much richer term in the ancient world than it is today. It implied unity in thought and purpose. To be a friend was to share all. Earlier, James said Abraham was called the friend of God because of his faith (James 2:23). Abraham was no faithless adulterer but was faithful to the one who called him. The one who is a friend to the world shares its outlook on life and feels very much at home in it.

"World" has many meanings in Scripture. Sometimes it refers to the creation (John 1:10; Romans 1:20). Sometimes it means the people of the world (John 1:29; 3:16). God, of course, loves his creation, especially humanity. Christians also are to be friends to creation and to their fellows. Many times, however, world refers to humans organizing themselves apart from God and his standards (John 8:23; 12:31). Christians must avoid being polluted by these worldly standards of worth (James 1:27; cf. 1 John 2:15-17). A person may thoughtlessly drift into worldliness, but eventually he confronts a choice; he can be a friend of the world or a friend of God. No matter how hard he tries to be popular and still be a Christian, the truth remains that he cannot serve two masters (Matthew 6:24).

4:5 Or do you think Scripture says without reason that the spirit he caused to live in us envies intensely?

Verse five presents two problems to the interpreter. The first is that James introduces a quotation with the words, "Scripture says," but the words that follow are not found anywhere in the Bible. Some have suggested they come from a lost book that James considered Scripture. Others think "Or do you think Scripture says without reason" is just a general statement on the authority of the Bible. Both of these suggestions are unlikely.

A third possibility is that these words introduce the quotation from Proverbs 3:34 found in verse six. The difficulty of this view is how to explain why James inserts the intervening words and why he repeats the phrase, "Scripture says" (in Greek, "it says"), before the Proverbs quotation.

The most likely explanation is that James is not quoting directly from Scripture in verse five but is paraphrasing one or more Old Testament verses. One cannot know which verses he paraphrases until one understands the meaning of verse 5b. That is the second problem with interpreting this verse.

Some scholars and translators believe that God is the subject of the verse. Thus the New Revised Standard Version translates: "Or do you suppose that it is for nothing that the scripture says: 'God yearns jealously for the spirit[2] that he has made to dwell in us'?" (cf. RSV). If this is the meaning here, then this could be a loose quotation from the Song of Moses where God is described as jealous of Israel because she has followed other gods (Deuteronomy 32:16, 21). This would fit well with the context of James. Like Israel, James's readers have committed adultery with the gods of the age (v. 4). Like a jealous husband (in the best sense of the phrase), God will not tolerate such unfaithfulness.

---

[2]This might mean the Holy Spirit, but if so, it would be the only reference to the Holy Spirit in James. More likely this is a reference to God giving the spirit (or "breath") of life to Adam (Genesis 2:7) and to the animals (Genesis 7:15). God demands human allegiance because he alone gives life.

The problem with this interpretation is that the Greek word for jealousy (φθόνος, *phthonos,* verb form ἐπιποθέω, *epipotheō*) is never used in the New Testament or in the Greek Old Testament to describe God (a different word is used in Deuteronomy 32). Only humans, not God, can commit the sin of jealousy or envy.

A better interpretation is that it is the human spirit that is prone to the sin of envy, as the NIV translates (cf. KJV, TEV, REB). In this case, the words may be a paraphrase of the Noah story in Genesis 6:5 and 8:21 where God says of man, "Every inclination of his heart is evil from childhood."[3] In Noah's day the people had rejected God's spirit (Genesis 6:3), and so he destroyed them. James's readers had also rejected God by befriending the world. The evil inclination of their hearts is envy (v. 2). They too are under judgment. However, after the flood God shows mercy. God's mercy and grace are also open to the humble in James's day (v. 6).

This is not to imply that God gives humans an envious spirit and so is to blame for sin. Some interpreters avoid this problem by making the quotation itself a question: "The spirit he has caused to live in us does not desire jealousy, does it?" The point would be that God made humans to desire him and his commandments (Psalms 42:2; 84:2; 119:20, 131), not to desire to be envious of others.[4]

However, this interpretation is not necessary to protect God from blame, since James has already made it clear that human desire, not God, is responsible for temptation (James 1:13-15). God gives life or spirit to humans, but they incline that spirit to evil. Jealousy is part of human nature, not the nature God gave in Eden but the nature that resulted from the Fall. James's point in the quotation is that just as people cannot master their tongues by their own power (James 3:8),

---

[3]See Lewis J. Prockter, "James 4:4-6: Midrash on Noah," *New Testament Studies* 35 (1989), 625-627.

[4]See Sophie S. Laws, "Does Scripture Speak in Vain? A Reconsideration of James 4:5," *New Testament Studies* 20 (1974), 210-215.

so they cannot control their jealous nature without help from God.

4:6 But he gives us more grace. That is why Scripture says: "God opposes the proud but gives grace to the humble."

God gives the help that human nature needs. He gives "more grace" or "a greater gift." However, that gift is only for the humble, not the proud, as James makes clear by quoting Proverbs 3:34.[5] First Peter 5:5 quotes the same passage to move his readers to humility. Although the necessity of humility is present in James, the primary emphasis of the quotation is on the grace of God.

4:7 Submit yourselves, then, to God. Resist the devil, and he will flee from you.

Yet the free gift of God can be accepted only through repentance and humble submission. James stresses to his readers the proper attitude for receiving God's grace with a series of imperatives. First, they are to submit (ὑποτάσσω, *hypotassō*, often found in military language) to God (Romans 10:3; Ephesians 5:24). Submission to God entails resisting the devil. "Resist" (ἀνθίστημι, *anthistēmi*) is another military word, similar to wars and battles (v. 1). Christians are not to fight with one another but take their stand against their true enemy, the devil (cf. Ephesians 4:27; 6:11-12; 1 Timothy 3:6-7; 1 Peter 5:8-9). By resisting "the prince of this world" (John 14:30), they are forsaking friendship with it (v. 4). Such resistance will prove successful. "The one who is in you is greater than the one who is in the world" (1 John 4:4). As Jesus made the devil flee at his temptation (Matthew 4:10-11), so Christians can vanquish the tempter through the power of Jesus.

4:8 Come near to God and he will come near to you.

One must resist friendship with the world but also must

---

[5]The entire section of Proverbs 3:19-35 is similar to the book of James.

embrace friendship with God. In the Old Testament, God called his people to worship by bidding them to "come near" (Exodus 19:22; Jeremiah 30:21; Ezekiel 44:13). However, at Sinai, the Israelites were warned not to approach too close to God (Exodus 19:21). It is a fearful thing to come into his presence. But the good news is God has chosen to come near to his people. In the Old Testament he came near to hear their prayers (Deuteronomy 4:7). In the New, the Word who was God became flesh and lived among us (John 1:14). No matter how far his people wander from him, even if they are unfaithful to him, he calls them back to him and promises to be near.

Wash your hands, you sinners,

But drawing near to God must be done with clean hands and a pure heart. "Washing the hands" might be meant almost literally here, if indeed the readers were allowing their envy to turn to murder (James 4:2). They were to wash the blood off their hands through repentance.

and purify your hearts, you double-minded.

However, washing the hands was a ritual of purification among the Jews, symbolizing purification of the heart. Only "He who has clean hands and a pure heart" can stand in the presence of the Holy God (Psalm 24:4; cf. Psalms 26:6; 73:13; 1 Timothy 2:8). The Pharisees condemned Jesus and his disciples for not washing their hands as their tradition taught. Jesus in turn condemns them because their hearts were far from God (Mark 7:1-8). To Jesus, it is the cleansing of the heart, not the hands, that is essential. Hands and heart stand for the whole person, both inward intent and outward action.

So here James is not encouraging a mere ceremonial washing of the hands but a purifying of the heart. As was discussed above (James 3:17), purity includes moral righteousness as well as singleness of intent. To be pure in heart is to reject the double-mindedness that James so often deplores (James 1:8; 3:9-12, 16). It is to abandon all attempts to befriend both God and the world.

4:9 Grieve, mourn and wail. Change your laughter to mourning and your joy to gloom.

To gain this purity requires repentance. Grieving, mourning, and weeping are the typical prophetic words for humbling oneself under the judgment of God (cf. Isaiah 22:4; 33:9; Jeremiah 4:28; 9:1, 18; 14:2; Lamentations 1:4; Ezekiel 7:27; Revelation 18:11, 15, 19). Repentance requires godly sorrow (2 Corinthians 7:10). Earthly laughter and joys must be set aside in light of the broken relationship with God. Laughter becomes mourning (cf. Luke 6:25). Joy becomes gloom.

The response of the penitent Christian is the opposite of the faithful Christian. For the one who trusts in God, trials and sorrows lead to joy (James 1:2-4). For one who has abandoned him, even joys become sorrow. The word for "gloom" here (κατήφεια, *katēpheia*) means to look downward. One is reminded of the penitent tax collector in the temple who would not look up to heaven but said, "God, have mercy on me, a sinner" (Luke 18:13). This is the picture of true repentance.

4:10 Humble yourselves before the Lord, and he will lift you up.

James may have this story of the tax collector in mind, for he quotes part of Jesus' statement at the end on the story: "For everyone who exalts himself will be humbled, and he who humbles himself will be exalted" (Luke 18:14b). Humility is the essence of repentance. It accepts the gracious hand of God who lifts the eyes of the sinner heavenward again.

Section Summary and Application:

In this, the heart of his epistle, James speaks to the contemporary problem of the worldly Christian. A great percentage of our population claims to be Christian. But what makes one a Christian? Are we Christians because we attend church and hear sermons? This is self-deception. Listening to the word is no good without obedience (James 1:19-20). Are we Christians because we believe certain things? Faith without action is dead (James 2:14-25). Are we Christians because we pray? No, even prayer can be evil if we pray for selfish pleasures. Do we claim to follow God while at the same time following the standards of the world? Then we are enemies of God.

An old television advertisement asked, "Who says you can't have it all?" James answers, "God says." One cannot be worldly and follow God. "Worldly" may conjure up memories of "Don't smoke, don't drink, don't dance" sermons, but worldliness is much more than specific vices. In an acquisitive society, it is considered normal to want more. Our whole economy is built on consumerism, ambition, and success. To be successful means fighting the corporate wars no matter who gets hurt.

To fit easily into such a society makes us friends of the world and its standard of pleasure. We cannot have the world and God (Matthew 6:24). He is a jealous husband who demands we keep our vows of exclusive loyalty to him. Keeping those vows are difficult in a culture where it takes little to be considered a Christian. James calls us to buck popular opinion. Such counter-cultural Christianity can be lived only by the grace of God. We turn to God in humble repentance, resisting the devil by rejecting the predominant values of our culture. Only then he will accept us back in spite of our unfaithfulness and lift us up to be with him.

XII. DON'T SPEAK AGAINST A BROTHER (4:11-12)

[11]Brothers, do not slander one another. Anyone who speaks against his brother or judges him speaks against the law and judges it. When you judge the law, you are not keeping it, but sitting in judgment on it. [12]There is only one Lawgiver and Judge, the one who is able to save and destroy. But you — who are you to judge your neighbor?

At this point James abruptly changes the subject to condemn slander. While this section has little contact with its immediate context, it is in line with James's warnings against anger (James 1:19-20), favoritism (James 2:1-13), cursing (James 3:9-10), and fighting (James 4:1-2). Having humbly received mercy from God, the readers must in turn show mercy to their brothers. God does not speak against his people but shows them grace. If they are truly pure in heart, they will not speak evil of others.

4:11 Brothers, do not slander one another.

James returns here to his usual greeting, "brothers," a far cry from calling them adulteresses (v. 4). Now he addresses them after their submission to God, reminding them that their relationship to him determines how they treat each other. Slander is condemned throughout the Bible (Leviticus 19:16; Psalms 50:20; 101:5; Romans 1:30; 2 Corinthians 12:20; 1 Peter 2:1). "Slander" is a legal term today, implying telling a falsehood that ruins another's reputation. The term here (καταλαλέω, *katalaleō*) is broader than that. Literally, it is "to speak against" or "talk down." One can tell the truth about others and still put them down. "Gossip about" might be a better translation, but only that gossip that results in harm.

Anyone who speaks against his brother or judges him

When one speaks of a brother in this way, one is judging him. Jesus said, "Do not judge, or you too will be judged" (Matthew 7:1; cf. Romans 2:1; 14:1-3). Unfair criticism and fault-finding are condemned here, not simply forming an opinion about someone. Jesus himself certainly talked against the Pharisees and warned his disciples against false prophets (Matthew 7:15). Paul called Elymas "a child of the devil" (Acts 13:10). Jude and other biblical writers speak harshly against false teachers. James himself has just called his readers adulteresses and enemies of God. It is not wrong to condemn others for their actions, if one does it out of love with hope for their repentance.

speaks against the law and judges it.

It is wrong to be overly critical, to put people down, to find fault in everyone. This is the gossip and judging James condemns. It is particularly nasty when directed at a brother or sister in Christ. To act this way is to speak against and judge the law. Likely James has in mind the royal law of loving neighbor as self (James 2:8 quoting Leviticus 19:18; this is why he uses "neighbor" instead of brother in verse 12).

When you judge the law, you are not keeping it, but sitting in judgment on it.

Critical gossip violates the law of love. However, it is much easier to see gossip in others than to admit one's guilt. It is as if one has decided that this law against slander applies to others, not to himself, and that he is above the law. This is not to keep the law or to be a doer of the word (James 1:22) but to sit in judgment upon it.

4:12 There is only one Lawgiver and Judge, the one who is able to save and destroy.

It is almost as if one thought he could give a better law than God. Such arrogance is beyond belief. God alone is the Lawgiver (cf. Exodus 24:12; Psalm 119:102; Isaiah 33:22). More frighteningly, he alone is Judge (cf. Psalm 7:11; 2 Timothy 4:8; Hebrews 12:23). All are in the hands of God. He can save (1 Samuel 2:6; 4:3; 2 Kings 5:7; Psalms 3:8; 17:7; 27:9; 72:13; 106:8; Isaiah 33:2; 60:16; Jeremiah 15:20; Zephaniah 3:17; Zechariah 9:16; 12:7; Luke 19:10), or he can destroy (Numbers 14:12; Deuteronomy 8:20; Isaiah 13:11; Jeremiah 25:9; Ezekiel 25:7, 16; Matthew 10:28). If James's readers do not want the one true Judge to condemn them, then they must not condemn each other (cf. James 2:12-13).

But you — who are you to judge your neighbor?

Christians should not presume to judge God or his law. To speak evil of a brother does both by violating the law of love. "Who do you think you are to judge your neighbor?" Paul uses a similar phrase against those who would assume the place of God (Romans 14:4).

Section Summary and Application:

We live in a critical, fault-finding society. The popular media are full of lurid exposés about celebrities. Criticizing others is such a part of daily conversation that it seems natural. James again challenges us to stand against our culture by refusing to harm others by our talk.

We also live in a tolerant society. "Don't judge me," has come to mean, "Don't criticize my lifestyle no matter how ungodly it is." James is not afraid to call sin by its name and condemn it strongly. Neither should we be afraid to stand for the right even if we are condemned as puritanical and narrow-minded. However, such condemnation must be made in love. We condemn sin in our brothers and neighbors to move them to repentance, not to feel superior to them. If we condemn others to boost ourselves, we are judging them, and we should remove the logs from our own eyes first (Matthew 7:1-5).

We also live in time when many in the church think we can pick and choose which laws of God we will obey. "That passage really doesn't apply to me," we say. This is not obedience at all but rebelliously taking the place of the One Lawgiver and Judge. To obey is to do all his will, even if we do not understand, even if we do not agree with it, even when it does not come easy. To keep from slander does not come easy.

XIII. DON'T COUNT ON TOMORROW (4:13-17)

¹³Now listen, you who say, "Today or tomorrow we will go to this or that city, spend a year there, carry on business and make money." ¹⁴Why, you do not even know what will happen tomorrow. What is your life? You are a mist that appears for a little while and then vanishes. ¹⁵Instead, you ought to say, "If it is the Lord's will, we will live and do this

or that." ¹⁶**As it is, you boast and brag. All such boasting is evil. ¹⁷Anyone, then, who knows the good he ought to do and doesn't do it, sins.**

This section also has only a loose connection to the previous one. From the arrogant presumption of judging the Law and our neighbor, James moves to presumption about one's future. He gives yet another hypothetical example, the speech of traveling businessmen. James has already spoken of rich merchants who perish in the middle of their travels (James 1:11). Commercial travel was common in the ancient world. Priscilla and Aquila were an example of one couple who often migrated, at least in part, because of their work (cf. Acts 18:1-3, 18-21; Romans 16:3; 2 Timothy 4:19; 1 Corinthians 16:19).

4:13 Now listen, you who say, "Today or tomorrow we will go to this or that city, spend a year there, carry on business and make money."

To have a successful business requires planning. One decides when and where to expand the operation. The word here for "carry on business" (ἐμπορεύομαι, *emporeuomai*, from which we get "emporium") is used only one other place in the New Testament, 2 Peter 2:3, where it is associated with greed. James may be correcting those for whom business has become too important. They may not be those who are already rich, but those who want to be (cf. 1 Timothy 6:9). Their hunger for success leads them to measure wealth in terms of monetary profit, not in terms of ultimate reality.

4:14 Why, you do not even know what will happen tomorrow. What is your life? You are a mist that appears for a little while and then vanishes.

At one level, planning for business is necessary. At another, such planning is foolish, for tomorrow is out of our hands. "Do not boast about tomorrow, for you do not know what a day may bring forth" (Proverbs 27:1). One may plan, but one does not control life. Scripture often speaks of the brevity of life as a mist or smoke that quickly disappears (cf. Job 7:7; Psalms 39:5; 102:3; 144:4; Hosea 13:3). Since life is short, those in business should set their hopes on God, not "on the uncertainty of riches" (1 Timothy 6:17-19). This passage in James echoes Jesus' story of the rich fool who made his profits and planned to enjoy them, only to die that very night (Luke 12:13-21).

4:15 Instead, you ought to say, "If it is the Lord's will, we will live and do this or that."

James has an alternative for the speech of these businessmen; they should say with all their plans, "If the Lord wills." Jesus and the apostles frequently refer to the controlling will of God (Matthew 7:21; 12:50; 18:14; Mark 3:35; Romans 12:2; 1 Corinthians 1:1; Hebrews 10:36). Jesus taught his disciples to pray to the Father, "Your will be done on earth as it is in heaven" (Matthew 6:10). With tears and sweat as blood, Jesus prayed those words himself three times in Gethsemane (Matthew 26:39-44). The early Christians followed his example by using phrases such as, "The Lord's will be done" (Acts 21:14; Romans 1:10; 15:32; 1 Peter 3:17), "If it is God's will" (Acts 18:21; 1 Corinthians 4:19), "God permitting" (Hebrews 6:3; 1 Corinthians 16:7), and "I am confident in the Lord" (Philippians 2:24) when making their plans.

Greek philosophers such as Plato and Seneca also used such phrases: "If the gods allow." The difference is that Christians serve the living God who is sovereign over all his creation. Bowing to his will should not become a matter of simply saying the right words. James wants action more than words (cf. James 1:22, 26; 2:12, 16, 18; 3:13). It is good to say, "Lord willing" when one makes plans. It is better to mean it by living under his control at every moment.

4:16 As it is, you boast and brag. All such boasting is evil.

To be confident of one's ability to analyze the future and plan for it, without regard for the One who holds the future in his hands is sheer arrogance. James calls it literally "boasting in your arrogance." "Boasting" (καύχησις, *kauchēsis*) is not always a bad word in James. The poor brother can boast (NIV "take pride") in his high position (James 1:9). Mercy boasts (NIV, "triumphs") over judgment (James 2:13). However, boasting about future plans without considering God's will is evil (cf. Proverbs 21:24; Habakkuk 2:5; Romans 1:30; 1 John 2:16).

4:17 Anyone, then, who knows the good he ought to do and doesn't do it, sins.

James ends this section with a proverbial phrase that seems to stand alone with little connection to relying on God's will. This may be just a general statement against sins of omission (cf. Matthew 25:45-46; Luke 12:47). As such it would apply to saying, "If it is the Lord's will." If one knows it is right to depend on God, not on personal plans for the future, then one must act accordingly.

However, it is possible that these words have a more narrow application. "Doing good" in the Bible often means caring for those in need (Galatians 6:9-10). James is concerned with care for orphans, widows, and anyone without clothing and food (James 1:27; 2:15). He might, therefore, be warning against making plans for tomorrow not only without considering God's will but also without concern for the poor. "Do not withhold good from those who deserve it, when it is in your power to act. Do not say to your neighbor, 'Come back later; I'll give it tomorrow' — when you now have it with you" (Proverbs 3:27-28). One does not know what tomorrow holds, life is short, so one should do all the good he can today. To assume tomorrow will come is arrogant presumption before God. It is sin.

Section Summary and Application:

All businesses plan. Business planning itself has become a large industry. Experts try to spot trends, do feasibility studies and market analyses, and so predict the future.

This attempt to predict the future has even invaded the

church. Many churches now have five-year plans, do demographic studies, and try all kinds of techniques to market the church.

So what's wrong with planning, either for business or the church? Surely God wants us to be efficient and to have a vision for the future. James says the problem is that it is easy to get caught up in our own plans and strategies and forget that God is in control. Business, even church business, easily takes on a life of its own with committees, bureaucracy, charts and graphs. "If you do these things," we are told, "your business or church will grow."

But growth and prosperity in business and at church are in the hands of the Lord. "If the Lord wills," must be more than a pious phrase to us. It must become the focal point of our existence. It is so easy to confuse our will for ourselves and our churches with his will and to think we control our lives. James calls this arrogance. Instead we must rely on God. To pray in his will means we cannot leave any part of our life, not even our jobs, out from under his control. God is concerned with all the business of life. He wants every hour of every day, not just a few on Sunday.

So we make our plans, but they are always tentative. They are always subject to being changed by God. And as we wait to know his will for tomorrow, we do what we can to help others today.

JAMES 5

XIV. WARNING TO THE RICH (5:1-6)

¹Now listen, you rich people, weep and wail because of the misery that is coming upon you. ²Your wealth has rotted, and moths have eaten your clothes. ³Your gold and silver are corroded. Their corrosion will testify against you and eat your flesh like fire. You have hoarded wealth in the last days. ⁴Look! The wages you failed to pay the workmen who mowed your fields are crying out against you. The cries of the harvesters have reached the ears of the Lord Almighty. ⁵You have lived on earth in luxury and self-indulgence. You have fattened yourselves in the day of slaughter.ª ⁶You have condemned and murdered innocent men, who were not opposing you.

ª5 Or *yourselves as in a day of feasting*

Earlier James spoke of the rich fading like a wild flower in the heat (James 1:10-11). He also accused the rich of exploiting Christians, dragging them into court, and blaspheming the name of Christ (James 2:6-7). Those denunciations are mild compared to what James says about the rich in this section. The vehemence of his condemnation may lead contemporary readers to dismiss his words as too radical. "What does James have against the rich?" one might ask.

However, one must take these words seriously. To do so, it is important to remember the place of the poor and the rich in the Bible.[1] Ideally there were to be no poor in Israel, for

---

[1] See George Peck, "James 5:1-6," *Interpretation* 42 (July 1988), 291-296.

those with goods were to share with those without (Deuteronomy 15:4-11). However, Israel never achieved this ideal. Thus, God himself championed and blessed the poor (Deuteronomy 10:17-19; Psalms 35:10; 86:1-2; 107:41). The poor in the Old Testament particularly trusted God to care for them and so were righteous. The rich, by contrast, often relied on themselves and cheated or neglected the poor (Leviticus 19:13; Deuteronomy 24:14-15; Jeremiah 22:13). As a result they fell under God's judgment (Isaiah 5:8; Ezekiel 16:49; Amos 2:6-7; 5:11; 8:4-6). Since riches are unsure and are often a spiritual snare, it is better to be poor and pious than rich and worried (Proverbs 11:28; 15:16; 23:4-5; Ecclesiastes 5:13-16).

This attitude toward wealth continues in the New Testament. Jesus himself was poor (Matthew 8:20), as were many of the early Christians (1 Corinthians 1:26-29; 2 Corinthians 8:1-5). The poor and hungry are blessed with good news (Matthew 11:5; Luke 1:53; 6:20; 21:1-4) and told not to worry about food and clothing, for God will care for them (Matthew 6:19-21).

On the other hand, the rich are often condemned, especially in the parables. The rich man and Lazarus the beggar have their places reversed after death (Luke 16:19-31). The man who thinks he can enjoy his wealth is called a fool; he dies that very night (Luke 12:13-34). Jesus even says that it is harder for a rich man to be saved than for a camel to go through the eye of a needle. His disciples (both then and now) are astonished at such a pronouncement upon the rich (Matthew 19:16-30; Mark 10:17-31; Luke 18:18-30). Jesus says plainly, "Woe to you who are rich" (Luke 6:24a).

James's condemnation of the rich is in line with the witness of Scripture, especially the words of the prophets and Jesus himself. Generally, in the Bible the poor are righteous, and the rich are evil. This is a generalization and so is not true in every case. However, one must not ignore the special place given to the poor as those who rely on God and the clear warnings against the dangers of riches. The Law, the prophets, Jesus, and James all reverse the normal human assessment that riches are good and poverty bad.

5:1 Now listen, you rich people, weep and wail because of the misery that is coming upon you.

Is James here condemning rich Christians or those outside the church who persecute the righteous poor? The answer is "both." The poor should take heart that their oppressors will be judged by God at the last day. They should wait for that day patiently (James 5:8). However, this section begins in the same way as the last one ("Now listen," v. 13), so James is still addressing those who should say, "If it is the Lord's will." Thus he condemns the rich both inside and outside the church who neglect and cheat the poor. Those who plan their business dealings without considering God (James 4:13-16) are also likely to cheat others to gain their wealth.

James tells the rich to weep and wail. Weeping here is the same word as in 4:9 (κλαίω, *klaiō*) translated "wail" there in the NIV), but it has a much different setting. In 4:9, weeping is a sign of repentance and sorrow for sin. Here the rich weep in pain at the punishment they face from God. Weeping and wailing are the typical words the prophets use to describe those under God's judgment (Isaiah 13:6; 14:31; 15:2-3; 16:7; 23:1, 6, 14; Hosea 7:14; Amos 8:3; Zechariah 11:2; cf. Luke 6:25). They call that judgment "misery," "disaster," "calamity," "distress," "ruin," and "destruction" (Isaiah 47:11; 59:7; 60:18; Jeremiah 4:20; 6:7; Hosea 9:6; Joel 1:15; Amos 5:9; Micah 2:4; Habakkuk 1:3; Zephaniah 1:15).

5:2 Your wealth has rotted, and moths have eaten your clothes.

James uses a prophetic vocabulary. Beginning in verse two, he speaks of God's future judgment in the past tense (the "prophetic perfect tense"). His condemnation of the rich is so sure, it is as if it has already happened. In the parable of the sower, the thorny ground is one who has the word choked by the deceitfulness of wealth (Matthew 13:22; Mark 4:19). So

James says the rich have trusted in wealth that has rotted and cannot deliver the permanence it promises.

5:3 Your gold and silver are corroded.

In James 2:2-3, the rich person is known by his gold ring and fine clothes. Here the clothes are eaten by moths (cf. Job 13:28; Isaiah 50:9; 51:8). Gold and silver are precious metals, which means they are permanent and impervious to rust. Yet James says they have rusted (a better translation than "corroded"). Obviously both these phrases echo Jesus' warning not to lay up earthly treasure that is destroyed by moth and rust (Matthew 6:19-20).

Their corrosion will testify against you and eat your flesh like fire. You have hoarded wealth in the last days.

The rich were dragging the Christians into court (James 2:6). Now the situation is reversed. The rich are on trial, and their rusted gold and silver now testify against them (cf. Mark 6:11; Luke 9:5). Their wealth now counts against them because they hoarded it and did not share with those in need. First the rust eats their silver and gold, then it eats them like fire, referring to the fire of hell (cf. Matthew 25:41; 2 Peter 3:7; Jude 23). Hoarding wealth in the last days may refer to the foolishness of seeking riches in light of the coming end, like the rich fool (Luke 12:19-21). More likely, this should be translated, "You have hoarded wealth *for* the last days," that is, the day of judgment (cf. James 5:8-9). Since their wealth will testify against them in the judgment, this is equivalent to "storing up wrath" against themselves (Romans 2:5).

5:4 Look! The wages you failed to pay the workmen who mowed your fields are crying out against you.

The wealth the rich have hoarded is not even their own. They stole it by failing to pay their workers. The plight of day laborers in the ancient world was the same as in our own. If they did not receive pay at the end of each day, they did not eat. Thus one of the most severe social crimes was to defraud workers of their daily wages, for it could lead to their starvation (Leviticus 19:13; Deuteronomy 24:14-15; Jeremiah 22:13). In the New Testament it is proverbial that the worker deserves his wages (Luke 10:7; Romans 4:4; 1 Timothy 5:18). The rust of the money the rich have stolen from these workmen testifies against them (cf. Malachi 3:5).

The cries of the harvesters have reached the ears of the Lord Almighty.

The cries of these harvesters may result from the hunger they feel but more likely are cries to the Lord for help and vindication (cf. Genesis 4:10; Genesis 18:20-21; Exodus 22:22-24; Judges 3:9; 4:3; 6:7; Psalms 4:1; 18:41; 22:2; 28:1; Isaiah 19:20; Micah 3:4). The way they have been treated by the rich is a crying shame.

They cry to the Lord *Sabaoth*, the Lord of Hosts (NIV "Almighty") or the Lord of armies (cf. Isaiah 1:9; 5:7, 9, 16, 24, 19:4; Romans 9:29). God was the true leader of the armies of Israel (1 Samuel 17:45). He also leads the heavenly army of numberless angels (Psalm 103:20-21). The rich thought they could cheat these workers and get away with it because the poor have no one to defend them. On the contrary, the protector of the poor is the Almighty Lord of the heavenly hosts who hears their cry (Malachi 3:2-6).

5:5 You have lived on earth in luxury and self-indulgence. You have fattened yourselves in the day of slaughter.

Instead of treating their workers justly and even aiding those in need, the rich have lived in luxury and self-indulgence (cf. Ezekiel 16:49; Amos 2:6-8; 8:4-6; Luke 16:19; 1 Timothy 5:6). In a shocking metaphor, James says they have grown fat off the spoils of the poor, but it is like fattening animals for slaughter. The prophets often speak of God's judgment as slaughter (Isaiah 34:2, 6; 65:12; Jeremiah 12:3; Ezekiel 21:14-15). The New Testament word for hell, *gehenna*,[2] even comes

---

[2]See the comments on James 3:6.

from the Valley of Hinnom that Jeremiah calls "the Valley of Slaughter" (Jeremiah 19:6). Thus, the self-indulgent luxuries of the rich will be paid for in hell (cf. Luke 16:19-31).

5:6 You have condemned and murdered innocent men, who were not opposing you.

Verse six should be translated literally as, "You have condemned and murdered the righteous one; he does not oppose you." Each of these phrases is problematic. The first question is the identity of "the righteous one." Some believe this refers to Jesus who is often called "the Righteous One" (Isaiah 53:11; Luke 23:47; Acts 3:14; 7:52; 22:14; 1 Peter 3:18; 1 John 2:1, 29; 3:7). If so, James is blaming the rich, perhaps the powerful Jewish leaders, for the death of Jesus.

More likely, this noun is a collective singular, meant to include all the righteous or innocent (cf. Paul's use of "righteous" in Romans 1:17). This accusation better fits the context. The rich have murdered innocent people by depriving them of their wages.

The second half of the verse raises two questions. The first is related to the discussion above. Who is it who does not oppose the rich? If Jesus, then this refers to his non-resistance to those who condemned him to death (Acts 8:32-35; 1 Peter 2:21-24). If the innocent poor are intended, then they do not oppose the rich either because they are powerless or because they follow Jesus' teaching of turning the other cheek (Matthew 5:39; cf. Romans 12:19).

Secondly, it is possible that this phrase is not a statement but a question: "Does he not oppose you?" Again, if Jesus is the "Righteous One" in mind here, it would mean that Jesus opposes the rich. If the innocent workers, then they would oppose the rich by crying out to God for vindication. The best suggestion for this phrase goes back to James 4:6.[3] There, using the same verb (ἀντιτάσσω, *antitassō*), James says God opposes the proud. Here, he is saying the same thing in

---

[3] Luis Alonso Schokel, "James 5:6 and 4:6," *Biblica* 54 (1973), 73-76.

question form: "Should not God oppose you?"

Placing these possibilities together, the verse should likely read: "You have condemned and murdered the innocent; should not God oppose you?" This is a fitting climax to James's prophetic denunciation of the rich. They may prey off others now and live in splendor and luxury, but the Lord of Hosts will slaughter them in the last days.

Section Summary and Application:

With his strong language against the rich, one wonders what James would think of the wealth of the typical American church member. Most of us reject the charge that we are rich. The rich are those with more than we have. As a student of mine once said, in all sincerity, "We're not rich. We live in a two-story house. Rich people have three-story houses." Like this student, we might define a luxury as "one more than we have." If we have two cars, three is a luxury. If three televisions, four is what we want.

To understand this passage, we must first admit it is written to us. We are the rich. If you had money to buy this book, then your income is higher than the majority of people in the world. If you have more than two sets of clothes, if you own a house or a car, then compared to most humans, you are rich.

Is it a sin to be rich? Reading James, we might think so. However, James and the rest of the Bible do not condemn wealth in itself, but they do warn strongly of its dangers. The more we have, the more we want. Soon, if we are not careful, we are cheating others, hoarding our money, and failing to share with the poor.

In an acquisitive society such as our own, riches are considered an unmixed blessing. We are taught from infancy to be good consumers and help the economy. Spending money is fun. Shopping is entertainment.

In such a culture, how do we begin to free ourselves from the love of money? A first step is for us to stop celebrating the rich. When we find ourselves dreaming of wealth and what we would do with all that money, it might help us to read this passage from James to see the fate of most of the rich. Perhaps then we could pray (as in the *Book of Common Prayer*), "In all our time of prosperity, good Lord deliver us."

XV. WAITING FOR THE LORD (5:7-11)

⁷Be patient, then, brothers, until the Lord's coming. See how the farmer waits for the land to yield its valuable crop and how patient he is for the autumn and spring rains. ⁸You too, be patient and stand firm, because the Lord's coming is near. ⁹Don't grumble against each other, brothers, or you will be judged. The Judge is standing at the door!

¹⁰Brothers, as an example of patience in the face of suffering, take the prophets who spoke in the name of the Lord. ¹¹As you know, we consider blessed those who have persevered. You have heard of Job's perseverance and have seen what the Lord finally brought about. The Lord is full of compassion and mercy.

5:7 Be patient, then, brothers, until the Lord's coming.
While some of James's readers may have been rich and deserved the warning above, most were likely those who had been defrauded by the rich. James has said the rich would be brought low and the lowly will be exalted (James 1:9-10), and that the rich have hoarded wealth for the last days (James 4:3) His poor readers might well ask "How long will it be until the Lord of Hosts brings the justice of this great reversal of earthly roles?"

James answers, "Learn to wait." He returns to his usual address to them, "brothers" (vv. 7, 9, 10), as he did before after a strong admonition (compare James 4:1-10 to 4:11). He uses a different word here, "patience" (μακροθυμία, *makrothymia*), than he used earlier for "perseverance" (ὑπομονή, *hypomonē*) through trial (James 1:3-4, 12). There is only a slight difference in these synonyms, with "patience" implying quietly suffering without complaint and "perseverance" implying heroic endurance.

They are to patiently suffer and patiently wait for the Lord's coming (παρουσία, *parousia*). In the early church, *parousia* became a technical term for the Second Coming of Jesus that meant the judgment and the end of the world (Matthew 24:3, 27, 39; 1 Corinthians 15:23; 1 Thessalonians 2:19; 3:13; 4:15; 5:23; 2 Thessalonians 2:1, 8; 2 Peter 1:16; 3:4, 12; 1 John 2:28). Their current suffering is light in view of the Second Coming when all will be put right.

See how the farmer waits for the land to yield its valuable crop and how patient he is for the autumn and spring rains.

To urge them to be patient, James uses the example of a farmer waiting for his valuable crop. This example may have been suggested by James's earlier statement that his readers had received the word planted in them (James 1:21). As the farmer must wait for his crop, so Christians must wait for the implanted word to yield its final harvest of salvation when Jesus comes. The farmer must work hard but also rely on God to send rain. "Autumn and spring rains" is literally "early and late." In Israel there were two rainy seasons that must come for a good crop to result. God promised these rains to his people if they obey him (Deuteronomy 11:14; 28:12; Jeremiah 5:24; Hosea 6:3-4; Joel 2:23; Zechariah 10:1).

5:8 You too, be patient and stand firm, because the Lord's coming is near.

Christians, like the farmer, must wait patiently for the blessings of the Lord (cf. Psalm 37). They are to stand firm (literally "to strengthen their hearts," cf. 1 Thessalonians 3:13; 2 Thessalonians 2:17) for the ultimate blessing of the Lord's coming is near. Jesus and his disciples often said the kingdom was near (Matthew 4:17; 10:7; Mark 1:15; Luke 10:9, 11; Romans 13:12; Hebrews 10:25, 37; 1 Peter 4:7).

What did they mean? Many of the early Christians expected Jesus to return in their lifetime. Now it has been almost

2000 years since he promised to return. Can one still say Jesus is coming soon, and the end is near? Yes, for we do not know when he will come. Jesus himself did not know the hour, so he urges his followers to be alert and keep watch (Mark 13:32-37). Peter reminds those who were doubting the promise of his return, that "With the Lord a day is like a thousand years and a thousand years are like a day" (2 Peter 3:8). So to every generation, the coming is near. James did not know when Jesus would return, but he is right in reminding his readers that his coming is near.

5:9 Don't grumble against each other, brothers, or you will be judged. The Judge is standing at the door!

From the certainty of the Second Coming, James turns to a warning against grumbling (στενάζω, *stenazō*) against one another. When times are tough and one finds it hard to wait for the Lord, it is easy to turn against fellow Christians. One might be too pious to complain to God but not pious enough to keep from griping at a brother or sister. The coming of the Lord brings vindication to the oppressed but also judgment against the grumblers (Matthew 7:1; James 4:11-12). As the coming is near, so the Judge is at the door (cf. Matthew 24:33; Revelation 3:20).

5:10 Brothers, as an example of patience in the face of suffering, take the prophets who spoke in the name of the Lord.

The persecution of the prophets was proverbial to the early church (Matthew 23:37; Luke 11:49-51; 13:33-34; Acts 7:52; 1 Thessalonians 2:14-15; Hebrews 11:32-38). Like Jesus (Matthew 5:11-12; Luke 6:23), James gives them as an example of the blessedness of those that suffer patiently (cf. James 1:12).

5:11 As you know, we consider blessed those who have persevered. You have heard of Job's perseverance and have seen what the Lord finally brought about. The Lord is full of compassion and mercy.

They had also heard of the perseverance (ὑπομονή, *hypo-*

monē) of Job. This is the only place Job is mentioned in the New Testament. If one reads the book of Job, he seems an unlikely example of patience since he loudly complains to God. However, it is not quiet patience James has in mind here but heroic endurance.[4] Job endured all that Satan threw against him and still maintained his relationship with God.

James's readers knew Job's story and had seen (literally in Greek) "the end of the Lord." End here might mean both culmination and purpose. Job's sufferings did not last forever but came to an end. God also had an end or purpose in mind in causing Job to suffer. His suffering was not meaningless. In the same way, Christians may suffer now, but if they persevere, their troubles will end, and they will see their purpose. Thus, "end of the Lord" refers to the end of Job's story, as the NIV translates, "What the Lord finally brought about." Job sees the coming of the Lord God in the whirlwind (Job 38-41). As a result of God's coming, Job's prosperity is restored and even increased (Job 42:10-17). Christians wait for the coming of the Lord Jesus who will restore their fortunes.

Both the Lord God and the Lord Jesus (the word "Lord" is ambiguous here and can refer to either) are full of compassion and mercy. They do not want their people to suffer forever. They will mercifully end their suffering and bless them as Job was blessed.

Section Summary and Application:

Many Christians today seldom think of the Second Coming. Perhaps we find it difficult to believe the Lord's coming is near when it's been almost two millennia since his first appearance. More likely we don't look forward to a better world because we feel so at home in this one.

However, in times of sorrow, pain, grief, and injustice, we too long for the Lord to come. Yet things go on the way they

---

[4]See Christopher R. Seitz, "The Patience of Job in the Epistle of James," in *Konsequente Traditionsgeschichte* (Gottingen: Vandenhoeck and Ruprecht, 1993), 373-382.

always have. The rich get richer. The righteous suffer. We too may wonder, "How long must it be?" When we are discouraged by life, we may be tempted to blame others, to grumble, and even to give up. In those times, James calls us to patience and perseverance. Those who are truly God's people have never had it easy in this world. Just look at the prophets and at Job. Yet they did not give up but trusted in the One full of compassion and mercy. We must trust him, too.

XVI. DON'T SWEAR (5:12)

¹²**Above all, my brothers, do not swear — not by heaven or by earth or by anything else. Let your "Yes" be yes, and your "No," no, or you will be condemned.**

Again, James turns to the subject of speech. This time he is concerned with swearing or taking an oath. This section may be related to the suffering discussed above and the next section on prayer. One should patiently endure suffering by praying to God who generously heals, not by making rash vows to him to try to move him to help. More likely, this section on swearing stands alone.

5:12 Above all, my brothers,
James prohibits swearing "above all." It is unlikely that James considers swearing the greatest sin of all, or even the greatest sin of the tongue.[5] Instead, like other ancient writers, he uses the phrase "above all" as an introductory phrase to the end of the letter. Thus, it means "finally" or "in conclusion."

---

[5]For the argument that James does intend swearing as the worst sin of the tongue, see William R. Baker, "'Above All Else': Contexts for the Call For Verbal Integrity in James 5:12," *Journal for the Society of the New Testament* 54 (1994), 57-71.

do not swear — not by heaven or by earth or by anything else. Let your "Yes" be yes, and your "No," no,

James is quoting Jesus who also absolutely forbade swearing (Matthew 5:33-37). Swearing was taking an oath before God that one spoke the truth. In the Old Testament, oaths were required in certain situations (Exodus 22:10-11; Deuteronomy 6:13; 1 Kings 8:31). The Law prohibited taking the Lord's name in vain (NIV, "You shall not misuse the name of the Lord your God," Exodus 20:7), that is, of swearing by God and not keeping the oath (cf. Leviticus 5:4; 19:12; Numbers 30:3-5; Deuteronomy 5:11; 23:21; Psalms 24:4; 63:11; Isaiah 65:16; Jeremiah 12:16; Zechariah 5:3-4; 8:17). Oaths were such a part of Old Testament life that God even swears by himself to keep his word (Genesis 22:16; Exodus 13:5; Number 14:16; Deuteronomy 1:8; 4:31; 7:8; Psalm 105:9; Isaiah 65:16; cf. Hebrews 6:13-18; 7:21).

By the time of the prophets, swearing falsely had become a widespread problem (Jeremiah 5:2; Hosea 4:15). Some were avoiding the responsibility of keeping an oath by swearing by something less than God — heaven, earth, Jerusalem, etc. To fight this misuse of oaths, Jesus (and later James) seems to forbid all swearing, commanding instead that "Yes" mean yes, and "No" mean no.

or you will be condemned.

Does this passage prohibit all swearing, even in law courts? Are all vows, even marriage vows, wrong? No, for Jesus himself spoke under oath at his trial (Matthew 26:63-64). God is often called upon to witness to the truth of Paul's statements (Romans 1:9; 2 Corinthians 1:23; Galatians 1:20; Philippians 1:8; 1 Thessalonians 2:5,10). It is not oaths but honesty at stake here. Christians should be truthful, people of their word, in all their dealings. They should not have to resort to swearing to convince others. Their character alone should be enough to prove their veracity. To have to resort to swearing puts one in jeopardy of judgment (cf. Matthew 12:34-37).

Section Summary and Application:
Honesty is in short supply today. Instead of our word being our bond, we cannot transact any significant business without a detailed legal contract. Even they are often broken or avoided through loopholes in the fine print. James calls us to be people of integrity. What we say can be believed by all. If we promise to do something, it will be accomplished. If we deny our guilt, then we are blameless. Again, it is only with God's help that we can reach this ideal of honesty and stand against the standards of our age.

XVII. PRAYER, CONFESSION, AND SAVING THE SINNER (5:13-20)

[13] Is any one of you in trouble? He should pray. Is anyone happy? Let him sing songs of praise. [14] Is any one of you sick? He should call the elders of the church to pray over him and anoint him with oil in the name of the Lord. [15] And the prayer offered in faith will make the sick person well; the Lord will raise him up. If he has sinned, he will be forgiven. [16] Therefore confess your sins to each other and pray for each other so that you may be healed. The prayer of a righteous man is powerful and effective.

[17] Elijah was a man just like us. He prayed earnestly that it would not rain, and it did not rain on the land for three and a half years. [18] Again he prayed, and the heavens gave rain, and the earth produced its crops.

[19] My brothers, if one of you should wander from the truth and someone should bring him back, [20] remember this: Whoever turns a sinner from the error of his way will save him from death and cover over a multitude of sins.

5:13 Is any one of you in trouble? He should pray.
James teaches his readers how to react to the changing circumstances in life. "In trouble" is actually "suffering" (as the prophets, v. 10). This is a general word for all hardships.

What should a Christian do when suffering? He should not blame God for trouble (James 1:13) but pray to him who gives all good gifts (James 1:17). That prayer might be for relief from pain or for patience in suffering.

Is anyone happy? Let him sing songs of praise.

What if things are going well? How does one show joy and cheerfulness? James says the best expression for emotion is praise in song. "Sing" (ψάλλω, *psallō*) is to sing a psalm, not necessarily one of the biblical Psalms but a composition of praise to God. When joyful, Christians give thanks to the one who gives true happiness (Ephesians 5:19-20).

5:14 Is any one of you sick? He should call the elders of the church

James returns to a particular form of trouble, sickness. When sick, one should call for the elders of the church. Certain Jewish leaders were called elders in the Old Testament (Exodus 19:7; 24:1; Leviticus 4:15; Numbers 11:16; 16:25; Deuteronomy 31:9; Judges 21:16; 2 Samuel 17:4) and the New Testament (Matthew 15:2; 26:3; Luke 22:52; Acts 4:5; 6:12; 23:14; 25:15). The early church used the same name for its leaders (Acts 11:30; 14:23; 1 Timothy 5:17, 19; Titus 1:5-9; 1 Peter 5:1; 2 John 1; 3 John 1). James himself is associated with the elders of the church in Jerusalem (Acts 15:2, 13, 23; 16:4; 21:18).

Although "elders" (πρεσβύτεροι, *presbyteroi*) means "older men," James intends official church leaders, not all older men here, since he calls them "elders of the church." The only other time this exact phrase is used, it refers to the Ephesian elders, obviously church leaders, whom Paul summons to Miletus. Why should the sick call for the elders, instead of others? Because they represent the entire church, and they are known as righteous men, the kind whose prayers are powerful (James 5:16b).

to pray over him and anoint him with oil in the name of the Lord.

When the elders come, they pray over and anoint the sick

with oil. Pray "over" (ἐπί, *epi*) may be meant literally; they stand over the sick bed. Or it might simply mean pray about the sick person. Anointing with oil does not seem to be a new practice James is advocating, but one with long standing. The use of oil in this passage has stirred great controversy. This verse does not support the Roman Catholic practice of Extreme Unction, for the sick here expect to be raised up, not to die. So why does James call for the sick to be anointed with olive oil? There are four major explanations.

Some say oil here is medicinal (cf. Isaiah 1:6; Luke 10:34). James is saying, "Take your medicine and pray, too." However, if the oil is strictly medicinal, why call for the elders to apply it? Why take medicine "in the name of the Lord?" Besides, oil was more like first aid in the ancient world, not a cure-all. It is an unlikely metaphor for all medicine. Finally, James says it is the prayer, not the oil, that heals (5:15).

Jews sometimes used oil in casting out demons. Jesus' disciples did the same (Mark 6:13). Is an exorcism intended here? The anointing is done "in the name of the Lord" as exorcisms were done (Acts 19:13). But if James intends exorcism, he does not make it clear; there is no hint of demon possession in this passage.

From Mark 6:13, others conclude the oil was used as a channel of blessing for one with the charismatic gift of healing "in the name of the Lord" (Acts 3:6; 4:10; cf. 1 Corinthians 12:9). However, James does not say, "call the elder who is the healer," but "call the elders of the church." Charismatic healing is probably not meant here.

Finally, oil symbolically stood for the special favor and blessing of God. Prophets (Isaiah 61:1), priests (Exodus 29:7), and kings (1 Samuel 10:1) were all anointed with oil to show that God was with them. In this verse, oil symbolizes the blessing of healing from God. Again, this is not magical healing oil. It is given "in the name of the Lord" (cf. James 5:10). The healing that comes from the anointing and prayer of the elders is miraculous, from the Lord, even if it is not charismatic. The oil does not heal; the Lord who hears prayer does (v.15). The oil is a symbol of his blessing.[6]

However, one should not be too quick to dismiss the power of that symbol. In the Lord's Supper, the bread and fruit of the vine are symbolic of Christ's body and blood. In baptism, burial in water is symbolic of dying and rising with Christ. Although these are symbols, they are not *mere* symbols that can be dispensed with. In the same way, the practice of anointing with oil as a symbol of the power of prayer perhaps should be revived in the church.

5:15 And the prayer offered in faith will make the sick person well;

The prayer of the elders for healing must be offered in faith, not like the doubting prayer of the double-minded person (James 1:6-8). Three promises are here made to faithful prayer. First, it will (literally in Greek) "save the sick." "Save" is intentionally ambiguous here. It can mean that prayer "will make the sick person well" (NIV). It is also the word used for salvation from sin (see v. 15b). Faith without deeds is dead, but an active faith saves (James 2:14). In a particular situation, it may not be the will of God to cure the sick. But if he does not grant them physical health, he will give them spiritual salvation.

the Lord will raise him up.

The second promise, "the Lord will raise him up," is also capable of two meanings. The Lord might raise him from his sick bed. If that is not his will, he has promised to raise his children from the dead.

If he has sinned, he will be forgiven.

Forgiveness of sins is the third promise. Sin is associated with sickness in the Bible (cf. Deuteronomy 28:58-62). If one sins, sickness may result. However, it is not a simple equation.

---

[6]For a summary of these positions on the meaning of oil, and arguments for the latter position, see Gary S. Shogren, "Will God Heal Us — A Re-Examination of James 5:14-16a," *Evangelical Quarterly* 61 (1989), 99-108.

Sickness is not always the result of sin. That was the mistake of Job's friends. Since he was sick, they assumed he had sinned (Job 8 and 22). In reply, Job maintained his innocence (Job 9:13-21; 13:18-14:22; 21:4-26; 29:1-30:3). Jesus' disciples also assumed that a man was blind from birth as a result of his or his parents' sin. Jesus corrects their error: "Neither this man nor his parents sinned . . ." (John 9:3). So, James says, "*If* he has sinned, he will be forgiven." Sickness and sin are not equated, but they are similar. The Bible is concerned with both physical health and spiritual health. Jesus sometimes forgave the sins of the sick before he healed their bodies (Luke 5:20-25). In verse 16, James even speaks of forgiveness as healing.

5:16 Therefore confess your sins to each other and pray for each other so that you may be healed.

Forgiveness, however, depends on confession and intercession (1 John 1:9). James may still have the visit of the elders in mind. The sick should confess their sins to their spiritual leaders. However, it is more likely that mutual confession by all Christians is intended. This may be done in a public assembly but also with individual brothers and sisters in whom they have confidence.

The prayer of a righteous man is powerful and effective. 5:17 Elijah was a man just like us. He prayed earnestly that it would not rain, and it did not rain on the land for three and a half years. 5:18 Again he prayed, and the heavens gave rain, and the earth produced its crops.

James summarizes his thoughts on prayer by saying it is powerful and effective when done by the righteous. To illustrate, he gives Elijah as one righteous man whose prayers were answered. Elijah was an exalted figure among the Jews (cf. Malachi 4:5-6). With Moses, he appeared in glory to Jesus at the Transfiguration (Matthew 17:1-8; Mark 9:2-8; Luke 9:28-36).

James brings the example of Elijah down to earth by reminding his readers that he was as human as they were. The

Old Testament does not mention Elijah's prayer to stop the rain (instead he takes an oath, 1 Kings 17:1). It does mention his prayer for rain (1 Kings 18:41-45). This verse does not mean God will grant all the requests of the righteous, for he did not give Elijah all he prayed for (see 1 Kings 19:4). It is a call for confidence in the power of prayer, or better still, confidence in the power of the Lord to whom we pray.

5:19 My brothers, if one of you should wander from the truth

Praying for one another leads to physical and spiritual healing (v. 16). Prayer might also lead a brother back to God. A brother may have wandered away like the one lost sheep among a hundred (Matthew 18:12-13; 1 Peter 2:25). The Greek word for "wander" (πλανάω, *planaō*) is translated "be deceived" in James 1:16. Through deception, the brother has wandered from the word of truth that gave him spiritual birth (cf. James 1:18). Apostasy in Scripture always includes what one believes and how one acts (for examples, see the commentary on Jude). The brother has committed more than a mere intellectual error. He has left the path of right living.

and someone should bring him back,

James calls his readers to act like the Good Shepherd and bring the brother back to God (cf. Matthew 18:10-17). "Bring him back" (ἐπιστρέφω, *epistrephō*) is actually "turn him back" (as in v. 20). Turning to God and away from sin is a favorite phrase for repentance in the Prophets (Isaiah 6:10; 55:7; Ezekiel 18:30-32; 33:11; Haggai 2:17; Malachi 2:6) and in the New Testament (Matthew 13:15; Luke 1:16-17; 22:32; Acts 3:19; 9:35; 11:21; 2 Corinthians 3:16; 1 Thessalonians 1:9). A true Christian is never concerned solely for his own salvation. He has the responsibility and privilege of winning back his erring brother (cf. Galatians 6:1; 1 Thessalonians 5:14; 2 Thessalonians 3:15; 2 Timothy 2:25; 1 John 5:16; Jude 22-23).

5:20 remember this: Whoever turns a sinner from the error

of his way will save him from death and cover over a multitude of sins.

Turning a brother from error results in "saving a soul from death." Probably spiritual death because of sin (as in James 1:15) is intended here. It also will "cover over a multitude of sins." Covering sin is a metaphor for forgiveness (Psalms 32:1; 85:2; Proverbs 10:12; Romans 4:7; 1 Peter 4:8).

But who will be saved from death, the one turning his brother or the brother who is turned? Whose sins are forgiven, the turner or the turned? There are passages that speak of salvation for one who warns his brothers (Ezekiel 3:18-21; 33:7-9; Daniel 12:3; 1 Timothy 4:16). However, "save him from death" sounds more like the penitent apostate is meant. Some grant that salvation from death applies to the corrected brother but think it is the converter who has his sins covered. Although this is possible, it seems more likely that both being saved from death and having his sins covered are blessings to the penitent brother. If he turns from error, God will save him, no matter how far he has wandered or how many sins he has.

James is not the only New Testament book that ends abruptly (cf. Acts, 1 John, and Mark, if the shorter ending in 16:8 is original). However, this ending may not be so abrupt after all, if James intends these last two verses to be a summary of his reason for writing. Like his beloved brothers, he too has tried in his letter to turn wanderers away from the world and back to God.

Section Summary and Application:

Our contemporary, scientific outlook can blind us to the power of prayer. We may think that medical science will eventually cure all disease. We may pray that God will guide the hand of the surgeon but doubt he can or will heal without the surgeon's skill. James says prayer in the name of the Lord heals and saves. This is one of the strongest encouragements to prayer found in Scripture. When faced with trouble, we pray to God. When sickness comes, it is fine to call the doctor, but we should call the elders, too.

We also should confess our sins to one another. If churches today had the closeness of the early Christians, we would not be so reluctant to be honest with one another about our shortcomings. We have the privilege of praying to God on behalf of our brothers and sisters. We can also ask them to pray for us. If we do pray for healing and forgiveness, we will find our prayers, like Elijah's, both effective and powerful.

Praying for others might even mean correcting them from deception and apostasy. This is not a call to feel spiritually superior. Such an attitude would violate James's warnings against slandering and judging our brothers. It is a call to care as much for our brother's soul as we do for his body. We pray for his delivery from physical death. We should turn him from a worse death. No one is beyond the love of God. Even a multitude of sins cannot separate us from him, if we humbly turn and follow.

THE BOOK OF
JUDE

INTRODUCTION

One writer calls Jude "the most neglected book in the New Testament."[1] One seldom hears sermons, Bible classes, or devotional readings from the book. Part of this neglect may be due to the brevity of the letter. Many Christians have trouble finding it tucked between 3 John and Revelation. It may be neglected because most of its content is also found in 2 Peter. The strangeness of the letter itself also explains its obscurity in the church. Jude quotes from books not found in the Bible. Even many of his biblical allusions are to lesser known Old Testament stories.

In spite of its strangeness, Jude has a powerful message for the contemporary church. In a culture that is increasingly apathetic or even antagonistic toward the Christian faith, in an era when pluralism and acceptance are the only ultimate virtues, we need to hear Jude's reminder that there are times the faith must be defended. In Jude's day as well as our own, that defense calls us to oppose false teaching, to live lives of faith and love, to pray in the Spirit, and to save those who falter.

AUTHORSHIP

The author calls himself "Jude, a servant of Jesus Christ and a brother of James." Jude or Judas is a form of Judah, one of the sons of Jacob and the tribes of Israel. There are four men named Jude (or Judas) mentioned in the New Testament who might be the author of the letter.

---

[1]Douglas J. Rowston, "The Most Neglected Book in the New Testament," *New Testament Studies* 21 (1975), 554-563.

1. Jude, the brother of Jesus. Mark 6:3 lists four brothers of Jesus, including James and Jude. For more on the brothers of Jesus, see the Introduction to James.

2. Jude, the apostle. In Luke 6:16 and Acts 1:13, he is called "Judas of James." The usual Greek usage (as reflected in most English versions including the NIV) is to translate this, "Judas son of James." If it means "brother of James," it might be a reference to the author of this letter. However, the author of Jude does not call himself an apostle and even quotes the apostles in a way that implies he is not of their number (v. 17).

3. Judas Barsabbas. He is briefly mentioned in Acts 15:22. He may have been a co-worker of James in Jerusalem. If so, "brother of James" would mean Christian brother, not physical brother. Although possible, this use of "brother of" is unlikely.

4. Judas of Damascus. After his vision on the road, Saul stays with him in Damascus (Acts 9:11). We are not sure he is even a believer. Even if he is, he is too obscure a figure to write an authoritative letter to a church.

Besides these four, there are two other possibilities followed by certain scholars.

5. It is written by an unknown Jude, brother to an equally unknown James. Of course, this is possible but seems unlikely.

6. It is pseudonymous, that is, written by an anonymous writer who uses the name Jude to enhance the authority of his writing. Although this practice was known in the ancient world, particularly among students of famous philosophers, no proven pseudonymous letters have been found. The primary argument for pseudonymous authorship is that the Greek of Jude is too good to be written by a Palestinian peasant. However, there is some question as to the high literary quality of the letter; the vocabulary is advanced, but the grammar is fairly simple. More recent discoveries have also shown that first century Palestine was more heavily influenced by Hellenistic Greek culture than was previously thought. It was not out of the question for a resident of Nazareth to write good Greek.

A second argument for pseudonymous authorship is that certain passages in Jude sound as if they come from the late first or early second century, too late for the biblical brother of Jesus to have written them. For more, see the discussion below on the date of Jude.

Although one cannot be certain, it is most likely that the author is the brother of Jesus and of James. Until quite recently, most scholars held he was the author. The content of the letter is consistent with this position. The author is well respected, familiar with the Old Testament and Jewish tradition, and knows the teaching of Jesus.

DATE, OCCASION, SETTING

If Jude, the brother of Jesus, wrote the letter, then it must date somewhere between 55-80. If "brother of James" implies James was still alive, then it dates before 62.

Some think two passages in Jude point to a date later than the lifetime of the Lord's brother. Jude 3 speaks of the faith as a body of doctrine delivered to the saints, a situation (some say) that could not have existed before the end of the first century. However, Paul uses similar language when he writes, so it does not necessarily reflect a later time (see the discussion below on v. 3).

In the other passage, Jude urges his readers to "remember what the apostles of our Lord Jesus Christ foretold" (v. 17). The argument is that this implies the apostolic period was in the fairly distant past. However, the next verse reads, "They said to you . . . ," implying that Jude's readers had direct contact with the apostles. At best, the language is ambiguous and does not clearly indicate a late date.

The specific occasion for writing is to warn of false teachers who have crept into the church. It is impossible to identify these false teachers with any known heretical group in the early church. Some have suggested they follow an early form of Gnosticism. The early Christian leader Irenaeus (130-200) says Cain and Korah were heroes to some Gnostic groups, so perhaps Jude is refuting that position by using them as negative examples (v. 11). Denigrating angels (v. 8) and even Jesus (v. 4) may have been characteristic of some Gnostics. However, our knowledge of early Gnosticism is quite limited, so we cannot be certain that Jude's opponents are Gnostic.

It is wiser to stay with Jude's own description of his opponents. They have misunderstood grace and perverted it into license (v. 4). They are antinomian ("against law"). They believe they are so advanced spiritually (perhaps as evidenced by their dreams and visions, v. 8) that they no longer are subject to God's law. Thinking themselves free from all moral restraint (v. 8), they pollute their bodies (v. 8), care only for themselves (v. 12), and end up like unreasoning animals (v. 10). These specific charges indicate Jude is fighting actual false teachers who have infiltrated a congregation, and he is not simply talking of heretics in general.[2] The false teachers he describes are similar to those in the Pastoral Epistles (1 Timothy 1:6-7, 19; 4:1, 7; 6:3-5, 20; 2 Timothy 1:13; 2:14, 16, 25; 3:1, 13; 4:3-4; Titus 1:10, 16; 3:9) and the Epistles of John (1 John 2:18, 22, 26; 4:1; 2 John 7; 3 John 9).

We have no clear indication of the location of Jude or of the church to whom he writes. Some scholars suggest a setting in Alexandria, Egypt;[3] others, Syria or Palestine.

RELATION TO 2 PETER

Jude 4-16 and 2 Peter 2:1-18 are so similar that one must

---

[2]See Stephan J. Joubert, "Persuasion in the Letter of Jude," *Journal for the Study of the New Testament* 58 (1995):75-87. However, Frederik Wisse, "The Epistle of Jude in the History of Heresiology," in Martin Krause, ed., *Essays on the Nag Hammadi Texts in Honour of Alexander Bohlig* (Leiden: E.J. Brill, 1972), p. 142, argues "The author is not trying to combat heresies within the church. . . . The author's purpose is to inform Christians everywhere that the enemies of the last days have arrived."

[3]John J. Gunther, "The Alexandrian Epistle of Jude" *New Testament Studies* 30 (1984), 549-562.

account for them in one of the following ways:

1. Coincidence. While possible, the extent of the similarity makes this unlikely. Of course, God could have inspired them both separately to write this way; but since inspiration is not dictation, one of the explanations below seems more likely.

2. They each independently use another document. If so, the document has not survived. Since almost all of Jude is similar to 2 Peter 2:1-18, then Jude would have added little of his own work to the document he copied. This is unlikely.

3. Jude adapted 2 Peter 2:1-18. If so, he would have shortened what Peter said. Usually, however, later writers expand on their sources.

4. Jude was written first, and 2 Peter 2:1-18 is an expansion of Jude's material to fit a different situation. Again, one cannot be certain, but this seems most likely.

Since there are so many parallels to 2 Peter 2:1-18 in Jude, the commentary will not refer to those passages in lists of cross-references. Instead, the reader is urged to read Jude with 2 Peter open beside it.

JUDE'S USE OF NON-BIBLICAL WRITINGS

Jude 1:9 refers to the story of Michael the archangel disputing with Satan over the body of Moses. This story is not found in the Old Testament but in a book called *The Assumption of Moses* written early in the first century. Jude 1:14-15 quotes directly from the *Book of Enoch* (also known as *1 Enoch*), a work written by several authors in the second century B.C. These two books are part of what is called the pseudepigrapha, that is, writings attributed to but not actually written by famous persons of the Old Testament. Although other New Testament writers may have known these books and have been influenced by them, Jude alone quotes directly from one of them and identifies the quotation as a prophecy.

Through the centuries many Christians have been disturbed by the idea that Jude would quote from a non-biblical book. Tertullian (A.D. 160-220) and a few other early Christian writers argued that *1 Enoch* was inspired since Jude quotes it as Scripture. Jerome (A.D. 342-420) tells us that others rejected the inspiration of Jude because he quotes *Enoch*. Both conclusions are based on the unwarranted assumption that Jude is quoting *Enoch* as inspired Scripture.

However, other New Testament writers (as well as Jewish authors) quote non-biblical sources because their words are true and valuable, not because they consider them inspired. Paul quotes from three Greek poets, Menander (1 Corinthians 15:33), Epimenedes, and Aratus (Acts 17:28). He introduces another quotation from Epimenedes by calling him a "prophet" (Titus 1:12). Obviously Paul did not think the writings of Epimenedes were inspired; Epimenedes was a "prophet" in the sense that the Cretans accepted him as such, and the particular statement Paul quoted ("Cretans are always liars . . .") was true.

In the same way, Jude may have had great respect for the *Book of Enoch* and have considered its prediction of the coming one as a true prophecy without accepting it as inspired Scripture (just as Christians today quote C.S. Lewis or other authors to make a point without claiming they are inspired). His references to *The Assumption of Moses* and to the *Book of Enoch* should not lessen our respect for the authority of Jude. He quotes these writings because, like Jude, they teach that God will ultimately judge false teachers who lead others astray.[4]

LITERARY THEMES AND STRATEGIES

The central theme of Jude is judgment of false teachers. Jude is best understood as a Jewish-Christian apocalyptic writing. Apocalyptic literature focuses on the end of the world

---

[4]For more on why Jude quotes these writings, see Walter M. Dunnett, "The Hermeneutics of Jude and 2 Peter: The Use of Ancient Jewish Traditions," *Journal of the Evangelical Theological Society* 31 (September 1988), 287-292.

and final judgment. Jude's examples of judgment are drawn primarily from the Old Testament (Israel in the wilderness, Cain, Balaam, Korah) but also from other Jewish apocalyptic literature such as the *Assumption of Moses* and the *Book of Enoch*. Jude follows a commentary pattern as he cites these past examples and then applies them to the false teachers of his day.

Literarily, Jude is fond of grouping three related items:
>Called, loved, kept (v. 1).
>Mercy, peace, love (v. 2).
>Godless, change grace, deny Jesus (v. 4)
>Israel, angels, Sodom (vv. 5-7).
>Pollute, reject, slander (v. 8).
>Cain, Balaam, Korah (v. 11).
>Clouds, trees, waves (vv. 12-13).
>Faith, love, hope (vv. 20-21).
>Be merciful, snatch from fire, show mercy (vv. 22-23).
>Before all ages, now, forevermore (v. 25)

He also contrasts his readers with the false teachers through the repeated use of two phrases: "dear friends" for his readers (vv. 3, 17, 20), and "these men" or "certain men" for the false teachers (vv. 4, 8, 10, 12, 14, 16, 19).

OUTLINE

I. ADDRESS AND GREETING — 1-2

II. REASON FOR WRITING — 3-4

III. JUDGMENT OF THE UNGODLY — 5-19
    A. Three Biblical Examples of Ungodliness — 5-7
    B. Application of Examples to Jude's Opponents — 8-10
    C. Three Further Biblical Examples of Ungodliness — 11
    D. Metaphors from Nature Applied to the Ungodly — 12-13
    E. Enoch's Prophecy Against the Ungodly — 14-16
    F. The Warning of the Apostles — 17-19

IV. A CALL TO FAITH, LOVE, AND MERCY — 20-23

V. DOXOLOGY — 24-25

BIBLIOGRAPHY
JUDE

Bauckham, Richard J. *Jude, 2 Peter.* Word Biblical Commentary. Waco: Word, 1983.

————. *Jude and the Relatives of Jesus in the Early Church.* Edinburgh: T&T Clark, 1990.

Bigg, Charles. *A Critical and Exegetical Commentary on the Epistles of St. Peter and St. Jude.* International Critical Commentary. Edinburgh: T&T Clark, 1901.

Charles, J. Daryl. *Literary Strategy in the Epistle of Jude.* London: Associated University Presses, 1993.

Chester, Andrew, and Martin, Ralph P. *The Theology of the Letters of James, Peter, and Jude.* New Testament Theology. Cambridge: Cambridge University Press, 1994.

Cranfield, C.E.B. *I & II Peter and Jude.* Torch Bible Commentaries. London: SCM Press, 1960.

Elliott, John H. *I-II Peter, Jude.* Augsburg Commentary on the New Testament. Minneapolis: Augsburg Publishing House, 1982.

Ellis, E. Earle. "Prophecy and Hermeneutic in Jude." In *Prophecy and Hermeneutic in Early Christianity.* Grand Rapids: Eerdmans, 1978.

Green, Michael. *The Second Epistle General of Peter and the General Epistle of Jude.* Tyndale New Testament Commentaries. Grand Rapids: Eerdmans, 1968.

Hiebert, D. Edmond. "Selected Studies from Jude," *Bibliotheca Sacra* 142 (1985), 142-151, 238-249, 355-366.

Kelly, J.N.D. *A Commentary on the Epistles of Peter and of Jude.* Harper's New Testament Commentaries. Peabody, MA: Hendrickson Publishers, 1969.

Kistemaker, Simon J. *New Testament Commentary: Exposition of the Epistles of Peter and of the Epistle of Jude.* Grand Rapids: Baker, 1987.

Kugelman, Richard. *James & Jude.* New Testament Message. Wilmington, DE: Michael Glazier, 1980.

Lucas, Dick and Green, Christopher. *The Message of 2 Peter & Jude.* The Bible Speaks Today. Downers Grove, IL: IVP, 1995.

Mayor, Joseph B. *The Epistle of St. Jude and the Second Epistle of St. Peter.* London: Macmillan, 1907.

Moffatt, James. *The General Epistles: James, Peter, and Judas.* Moffatt New Testament Commentary. New York: Harper and Brothers, n.d.

Neyrey, Jerome H. *2 Peter, Jude.* Anchor Bible. New York: Doubleday, 1993.

Osburn, Carroll D. "1 Enoch 80:2-8 (67:5-7) and Jude 12-13," *Catholic Biblical Quarterly* 47 (1985), 296-303.

_____. "The Christological Use of I Enoch 1:9 in Jude 14,15," *New Testament Studies* 23 (1977), 334-341.

Reicke, Bo. *The Epistles of James, Peter, and Jude.* Anchor Bible. New York: Doubleday, 1964.

Sidebottom, E.M. *James, Jude, 2 Peter.* New Century Bible Commentary. Grand Rapids: Eerdmans, 1967.

Watson, Duane Frederick. *Invention, Arrangement, and Style: Rhetorical Criticism of Jude and 2 Peter.* Atlanta: Scholars Press, 1988.

JUDE

I. ADDRESS AND GREETING (1-2)

¹Jude, a servant of Jesus Christ and a brother of James,
To those who have been called, who are loved by God the Father and kept by[a] Jesus Christ: ²Mercy, peace and love be yours in abundance.

[a] *1* Or *for*; or *in*

v. 1 Jude, a servant of Jesus Christ

Like most ancient letters, this one begins by identifying its author and recipients. The author's name in Greek is Judas, but it is traditionally translated Jude in English versions (perhaps to distinguish him from Judas Iscariot). The author is probably Jude, the brother of Jesus (see Introduction), but he calls himself a servant (δοῦλος, *doulos*, also translated "slave") of Jesus Christ. He does not claim authority to write because he is the earthly brother of the Lord, but because, like others (Romans 1:1, Philippians 1:1, James 1:1, 2 Peter 1:1), he is the slave of the Messiah.

and a brother of James,

He distinguishes himself from others named Judas by calling himself the brother of James. This is an unusual designation, since most Jews would use "son of" (*bar*) to describe themselves. This greeting shows how famous James, the brother of the Lord, was in the early church (see the section on the brothers of Jesus in the Introduction to James).

To those who have been called, who are loved by God the Father and kept by Jesus Christ:

Jude does not address his readers by name or location. It may be that his letter originally had such an address that was lost in copying. Some think Jude intended this to be a circular letter to be read in several churches since no specific destination is given. Thus, Jude has been called a "general" or "catholic" (that is, universal) epistle. However, the warmth of Jude's language toward his readers points to a personal knowledge of their particular situation. It is likely, then, that he writes to a specific congregation, not to a group of churches.

Jude does not greet his readers by name, but he does describe them in three ways: "called," "loved by God," and "kept by Jesus Christ." God's calling of his people is a rich concept in the Old Testament (Isaiah 41:9; 42:6; 48:12,15; 49:1; 54:6; Hosea 11:1) and the New Testament (Matthew 22:14; Romans 1:6-7; 8:28; 1 Corinthians 1:2,24,26; 2 Thessalonians 2:14; 1 Peter 1:15; 2 Peter 1:3, Revelation 17:14). "Called" (κλητός, *klētos*) means they have received God's gracious election through Jesus and are to live faithfully in light of that calling.

Jude also says they are loved (ἀγαπάω, *agapaō*) by God. Some accuse Jude of being exclusively concerned with false teaching. In fact, his main concern is to keep his readers in God's love (see Jude 21). Those loved by God are kept (τηρέω, *tēreō*) by (or for) Jesus Christ. This may mean they are protected by Jesus from evil, including the evil of false teachers (John 17:12). More likely, they are protected for Jesus; that is, they are kept safe for him to receive at his Second Coming (1 Thessalonians 5:23; 2 Timothy 1:12; 1 Peter 1:4-5; Revelation 3:10). The implication is that not all who are called stay with Jesus or are kept for him. Those kept for Jesus are contrasted with the angels who did not keep their place and so have been kept in darkness (Jude 6).

v. 2 Mercy, peace and love be yours in abundance.

Jude greets his readers with the words mercy, peace, and

love. Early Christians took the typical Greek greeting (χαίρειν, *chairein*, "greeting") and the typical Hebrew greeting (שׁלוֹם, *shalom*, "peace") and gave them deeper meaning. Paul usually greets his readers with "grace" (χάρις, *charis*) and "peace" (εἰρήνη, *eirēnē*), expressing his wish and prayer that God grant them those spiritual blessings.

Jude does not use "grace and peace," but "mercy and peace," a typical Jewish greeting. It is interesting that "mercy" (ἔλεος, *eleos*) also appears in the greetings in 1 Timothy 1:2; 2 Timothy 1:2; and 2 John 3, all books that warn of false teachers, just as Jude does. Mercy is especially needed in the face of danger from false teachers. Jude is the only New Testament writer to add "love" (ἀγάπη, *agapē*) to his greeting, again emphasizing the importance of love in this short letter (see vv. 3, 12, 17, 21).

II. REASON FOR WRITING (3-4)

³**Dear friends, although I was very eager to write to you about the salvation we share, I felt I had to write and urge you to contend for the faith that was once for all entrusted to the saints. ⁴For certain men whose condemnation was written about**[a] **long ago have secretly slipped in among you. They are godless men, who change the grace of our God into a license for immorality and deny Jesus Christ our only Sovereign and Lord.**

[a]*4 Or* men who were marked out for condemnation

v. 3 Dear friends, although I was very eager to write to you about the salvation we share,

Jude continues with this theme of love by calling his readers "beloved" (a better translation of ἀγαπητοί, *agapētoi*, than "dear friends"). He gives a glimpse of the letter he intended or perhaps even started to write. It would have been a general essay on "the salvation we share" (cf. Titus 1:4, "our common faith"). This may mean the salvation Jude and his readers had in common or may refer to the common salvation of Jews and Gentiles. In either case, Jude abandons his intended letter because he felt compelled by the presence of false teachers among those he loved to write a quite different kind of letter, an appeal to contend for the once-for-all faith.

I felt I had to write and urge you to contend for the faith

The word "contend" (ἐπαγωνίζομαι, *epagōnizomai*) originally had a military or sporting setting; one fought for victory on the battlefield or in the arena. Here it reminds one of the strenuous effort that must be made on behalf of the faith. Christians also are in a battle (Ephesians 6:10-13; 1 Thessalonians 5:8; 1 Timothy 6:12; 2 Timothy 2:4, 4:7) or a competition (1 Corinthians 9:24-25; 2 Timothy 2:5) against evil. Jude will later remind his readers that one fights for the faith not only by opposing false teachers but by prayer, mercy, and love (Jude 17-23). In the name of tolerance, contemporary leaders are prone to ignore all questionable teaching in the church. Jude says defending the faith and warning against false teaching can be a sign of love for our brothers and sisters.

Faith here refers to what is believed, not the act of believing. Some scholars think this objective use of faith proves that Jude was written after the time of the apostles, a time when Christian orthodoxy in doctrine became more fixed. However, other passages in the New Testament speak of faith as a set of doctrines that are believed (Romans 10:8; 1 Corinthians 16:13; 2 Corinthians 13:5; Galatians 1:23, 3:23-25; Philippians 1:25; 1 Timothy 3:9, 4:1,6), so Jude's use of faith does not argue for a late date for the letter.

that was once for all entrusted to the saints.

This message that they believed had been entrusted to them once for all. "Entrusted" or "passed on" (παραδίδωμι, *paradidōmi*) is similar to the word for tradition. This is an appeal to the past. They had received this message of salvation, the faith, from others; now they must fight to preserve it (cf. 1 Corinthians 11:2, 23: 2 Thessalonians 2:15; 3:6; 1 Timothy 6:20-21).

This message of faith was normative. It was not to be changed. Like Jesus' sacrifice for sin (Hebrews 10:2, 10; 1 Peter 3:18), it was once for all. Unlike the false teachers, Jude does not believe in a progressive development of Christian doctrine.

True faith had been passed on once for all "to the saints." In the early church, every Christian was a saint (Acts 9:13, 32, 41; Romans 8:27; 12:13; 15:25, 26, 31; Hebrews 6:10; Revelation 5:8). "Saints" (ἅγιοι, *hagioi*) literally means "holy ones." Christians are called to be devoted to God and live holy lives. This contrasts with the false teachers who deny Christ by their ungodliness.

v. 4 For certain men whose condemnation was written about long ago have secretly slipped in among you.

Jude feels compelled to urge the saints to fight for the faith because false teachers had slipped in among them. Like Paul (Galatians 1:7, 2:4; 2 Corinthians 10:10-12), Jude will not dignify these opponents of the faith by calling them by name; instead, he uses "certain men" or "these men" (Jude 8, 10,12,16,19). These men intended to deceive the church since they "secretly slipped in among you" (cf. John 10:1; Galatians 2:4; 2 Timothy 3:6). This may imply they were traveling missionaries who had come as strangers to the church and then lived off its generosity. If so, they are similar to the deceivers warned of in 2 John 10-11: "If anyone comes to you and does not bring this teaching, do not take him into your house or welcome him. Anyone who welcomes him shares in his wicked work."

Although the church may be caught off guard by these false teachers, they can't slip in past the God who knew of them and foretold their condemnation. That condemnation was "written about long ago," perhaps referring to Old Testament warnings against false prophets as well as to warnings from Jesus and the apostles. It probably also refers to the prophecy against false teachers from the *Book of Enoch* (see Introduction and commentary on Jude 14-15).

They are godless men, who change the grace of our God into a license for immorality

These false teachers are "ungodly" (ἀσεβής, *asebēs*, a word used six times in different forms in Jude). This implies moral as well as doctrinal fault. False teaching is not merely intellectual but has ethical implications. Specifically, these teachers change grace into a license for immorality (ἀσέλγεια, *aselgeia*). Not all change is good. This one is a perversion of the meaning of grace. Throughout the New Testament, Christians are warned against immorality (Romans 13:13-14; 2 Corinthians 12:21; Galatians 5:19; 1 Peter 4:3; 2 Peter 2:2, 7, 18; Revelation 2:20-24). The false teachers in Jude not only ignore that warning, they even believe they have the right to be immoral. To Paul's question, "Shall we go on sinning so that grace may increase?" (Romans 6:1), these men would answer with a resounding, "Yes!"

and deny Jesus Christ our only Sovereign and Lord.

This misunderstanding of grace as permission to sin leads them to "deny Jesus Christ our only Sovereign and Lord."[1] This denial was probably not verbal (if they had said "Jesus is not Lord," they could not have slipped into the church) but actual: "They claim to know God, but by their actions they deny him" (Titus 1:16). These false teachers wanted salvation without following the Savior who as Sovereign and Lord demands that we die to sin as we follow him.

III. THE JUDGMENT OF THE UNGODLY (5-19)

A. THREE BIBLICAL EXAMPLES OF UNGODLINESS (5-7)

⁵**Though you already know all this, I want to remind you that the Lord**ᵃ **delivered his people out of Egypt, but later**

---

[1]Some scholars think "the only Sovereign" refers to God the Father. If so, the false teachers deny both the Father and the Son. However, most likely the entire phrase refers to Jesus as in the NIV. See Bauckham, *Jude, 2 Peter*, pp. 39-40.

destroyed those who did not believe. ⁶And the angels who did not keep their positions of authority but abandoned their own home — these he has kept in darkness, bound with everlasting chains for judgment on the great Day. ⁷In a similar way, Sodom and Gomorrah and the surrounding towns gave themselves up to sexual immorality and perversion. They serve as an example of those who suffer the punishment of eternal fire.

ᵃ5 Some early manuscripts *Jesus*

Jude begins his look at Old Testament examples by saying he wants to remind his readers of what they already know. This may mean they know the errors of the false teachers. More likely it indicates they know their Bibles, that is, they are familiar with the examples he is about to cite. Much of the teaching of the early church, as well as of the current church, is not brand-new but is a reminder to Christians of what they already know or, at least, should know. The only "new truths" come from false teachers (cf. Galatians 1:9; 1 John 2:19-28). Those new teachings lead to a new morality, or rather to an old immorality.

v. 5 Though you already know all this, I want to remind you that the Lord delivered his people out of Egypt, but later destroyed those who did not believe.

Looking at each of the three examples of apostasy Jude gives will show what they have in common. His first example is Israel who was led by the Lord[2] out of Egypt but refused to enter the promised land and so was punished. This is the story of the twelve spies, ten of whom were afraid of the

---

[2]This is probably the Lord God, but some manuscripts read "Jesus" instead of "Lord." If "Jesus" is the reading here, it may refer to Joshua (another form of the name "Jesus") who led Israel from Egypt. If it is Jesus Christ who is intended here, then Jesus is identified with the angel of the Lord who led Israel. See Jarl Fossum, "Kyrios Jesus as the Angel of the Lord in Jude 5-7," *New Testament Studies* 33 (1987), 226-243.

inhabitants of the land while two, Caleb and Joshua, called for faith in God to give them victory. Most of the Israelites follow the ten, rebel against the Lord, and are punished for their unfaithfulness (Numbers 13:25-14:38). God destroys the very people he had rescued. It is the people of God, not outsiders, who are punished. No wonder this story is used elsewhere in the New Testament to warn Christians against apostasy (1 Corinthians 10:1-13; Hebrews 3:7-4:13).

v. 6 And the angels who did not keep their positions of authority but abandoned their own home —

The second example is the fall of the angels. Although some associate the fall of the morning star (Isaiah 14:11-17) and the king of Tyre (Ezekiel 28:11-19) with the fallen angels, those passages more likely refer to the destruction of human rulers. Some understand the sons of God marrying the daughters of men (Genesis 6:2) to refer to angels falling by marrying humans (see the discussion below). Most likely Jude is referring to the account of the fall of the angels in the *Book of Enoch* (see the Introduction to Jude for a discussion of his use of Enoch).

these he has kept in darkness, bound with everlasting chains for judgment on the great Day.

Although the Bible does not give details of the fall, it is clear the angels abandoned their proper positions and so deserve punishment (2 Peter 2:4). "Kept" (τηρέω, *tēreō*) in darkness may be a play on words. This is the same word Jude used to greet his readers in v. 2, "kept by Jesus Christ." Jesus keeps everyone in one of two ways, either in his loving care or in darkness for judgment. The chaining of the fallen angels does not contradict other New Testament passages that describe the devil and his angels as active in the world (Luke 22:31; Romans 8:38; Ephesians 6:12; 1 Peter 5:8; Revelation 20:1-3), but rather it points to the certainty of their punishment on "the great Day" of judgment.

v. 7 In a similar way, Sodom and Gomorrah and the surrounding towns gave themselves up to sexual immorality and perversion. They serve as an example of those who suffer the punishment of eternal fire.

The third example, Sodom and Gomorrah, is introduced by "in the same way" (ὡς, *hōs*) tying it closely to the angel example. Genesis 18-19 tells how God rained fire on Sodom and Gomorrah and the surrounding towns of Admah and Zeboiim (cf. Deuteronomy 29:23; Hosea 11:8) but saved Lot and his daughters. God destroyed the cities because of their great sin, referring to their homosexual practices (Genesis 19:5) and to their arrogant oppression of the poor (see Ezekiel 16:48-50). The "eternal fire" they suffer points to the lasting effects of their destruction and warns of the eternal fire of hell for those who follow their example (see v. 23).

What do these three examples have in common? In all three, evildoers are punished. The unbelieving in Israel are destroyed during the forty years of wandering in the wilderness, the fallen angels are bound in darkness for the judgment day, and Sodom and Gomorrah face eternal fire. So too the false teachers in Jude will receive their due punishment.

Some have tried to find a common sexual sin in all three examples. This is unlikely in the case of Israel, unless Jude's reference to "those who did not believe" includes their sin of "revelry" (sexual immorality) at Sinai (Exodus 32:6). If Jude thinks the sons of God in Genesis 6:2 are angels, then they commit sexual sin with the daughters of men. This forms a close parallel with Sodom where men desire to have sexual relations with angels (who are in the form of men, Genesis 19:1).

Although Jude may have chosen these three as examples of sexual sin, it is more likely he chose them because they speak of intentionally leaving God to follow another way of life. Israel is saved from Egypt "once for all" (v. 5, ἅπαξ, *hapax*, a Greek word inexplicably left untranslated by the NIV),[3] just as

---

[3]Perhaps the NIV puts *hapax* with the previous phrase, "You already (once for all?) know." However it makes more sense in the next phrase: "The Lord once saved them, but later destroyed them."

Jude's readers were entrusted with the faith "once for all" (same Greek word, v. 3). However, those Israelites who did not remain faithful were destroyed, just as Jude's readers will be if they do not fight to preserve their faith. The evil angels also abandoned their proper place and home. Sodom and Gomorrah literally "went after strange flesh," that is, they left their natural sexual desires.

These three are all examples of willful apostasy. All intentionally left their saved status to pursue an ungodly way of life. Their punishment is described in increasingly severe terms. The unbelieving Israelites are destroyed, the apostate angels are bound with everlasting chains, and Sodom and Gomorrah suffer eternal fire.

B. APPLICATION OF EXAMPLES TO JUDE'S OPPONENTS (8-10)

⁸In the very same way, these dreamers pollute their own bodies, reject authority and slander celestial beings. ⁹But even the archangel Michael, when he was disputing with the devil about the body of Moses, did not dare to bring a slanderous accusation against him, but said, "The Lord rebuke you!" ¹⁰Yet these men speak abusively against whatever they do not understand; and what things they do understand by instinct, like unreasoning animals — these are the very things that destroy them.

v. 8 In the very same way,

"In the same way" (ὁμοίως, *homoiōs*) compares the men troubling Jude's readers with the Old Testament apostates of Israel, the angels, and Sodom and Gomorrah. By making this comparison between such notorious sinners and the false teachers, "Jude intends to neutralize all possible sympathetic feelings toward them."[4]

---

[4]Joubert, 84.

these dreamers pollute their own bodies,

Jude calls these men "dreamers," possibly meaning they indulge in erotic fantasies and so "pollute their own bodies." More likely, this means they claim divine approval through dreams for their beliefs and practices. God did give revelations through dreams (Genesis 40:5-19; Judges 7:13; Matthew 1:20; 2:12-13; Acts 2:17 quoting Joel 2:28); however, the Israelites were warned against prophets and dreamers who would lead them into rebellion against God (Deuteronomy 13:1-5; Jeremiah 27:9).

reject authority and slander celestial beings.

Like Sodom and Gomorrah, these false teachers are not only sexually immoral ("pollute their bodies"), but they also show disrespect for angels and thus for God. The "authority" (κυριότης, *kyriotēs*) they reject is elsewhere translated "powers" (Colossians 1:16) or "dominion" (Ephesians 1:21), referring to heavenly beings or angels. They speak evil of "celestial beings" (δόξας, *doxas*, literally, "glories" or "glorious ones"), that is, of the angels in glory around God's throne.

This may mean they taught directly against angels but more likely means they rejected God's moral law that included prohibitions against sexual immorality, the "message spoken by angels" (Hebrews 2:2). False teaching always leads to immoral practice. They misunderstand grace by rejecting all law (that was brought by angels) and so turn grace into a license for immorality (v. 4). By so doing they, like Israel, the fallen angels, and Sodom and Gomorrah, reject the Lord and leave their proper place.

v. 9 But even the archangel Michael, when he was disputing with the devil about the body of Moses,

Their audacity is contrasted with the reticence of Michael the archangel, who did not take it upon himself to slander even Satan but relied on God's judgment. The story of Michael disputing with Satan over the body of Moses is not found in the Old Testament (for Moses' death, see

Deuteronomy 34:6). Instead, according to early Christian writers Clement of Alexandria (A.D. 150-215), Origen (A.D. 185-254), and Didymus (A.D. 313-398), Jude found the story in *The Assumption of Moses*, a book written early in the first century that today exists only in fragmentary form (see the Introduction for a discussion of Jude's use of non-biblical books).

did not dare to bring a slanderous accusation against him, but said, "The Lord rebuke you!"

Both Testaments (Daniel 10:13, 21; 12:1; Revelation 12:7-9) and Jewish intertestamental literature describe Michael as the great warrior archangel. If anyone had the right to rebuke the fallen angel Satan, it was Michael. But he knows God alone is Lord of the angels, so he says, "The Lord rebuke you!" (cf. Zechariah 3:2).

v. 10 Yet these men speak abusively against whatever they do not understand; and what things they do understand by instinct, like unreasoning animals — these are the very things that destroy them.

In contrast to Michael who has respect even for Satan's status as an angel, the false teachers slander what they don't understand. Through their dreams they claim greater understanding than others. However, they are not spiritually superior to other humans (as they claim) but are inferior in understanding. Since they don't understand the heavenly realms (although they claim to through their dreams), they have become merely animal in nature and so will be destroyed.

C. THREE FURTHER BIBLICAL EXAMPLES OF UNGODLINESS (11)

11Woe to them! They have taken the way of Cain; they have rushed for profit into Balaam's error; they have been destroyed in Korah's rebellion.

v. 11 Woe to them!

Frequently judgment is pronounced upon wrongdoers by "woe to you." These woe pronouncements occur most often in the Old Testament prophets and on the lips of Jesus (Matthew 11:21; 23:13-32; Luke 11:42-52).

They have taken the way of Cain;

Cain is a clear example of jealousy and murder (Genesis 4:1-16; 1 John 3:12) but may seem an unlikely warning against false teaching. However, there is a strong rabbinical tradition, also found in the Jewish writer Philo (20 B.C.–A.D. 50), that portrays Cain as the first heretic. His way is that of selfishness and sensuality. If this tradition is not in Jude's mind, perhaps the comparison is that the false teachers are harming their brothers by their doctrines as Cain harmed his brother Abel. Heresy is always more than being sincerely mistaken about a doctrine. As with Cain, it is direct disobedience to God and has harmful consequences for others.

they have rushed for profit into Balaam's error;

There are two Balaam stories in the Old Testament. In the first (Numbers 22-24), he is hired by Balak, king of Moab, to curse Israel. However, Balaam refuses to curse and blesses them instead. In the second story, Balaam leads Israel into sexual immorality and idolatry (Numbers 25:1-3; 31:16). The parallels with these false teachers are many. Like Balaam, they claim to be prophets ("dreamers" v. 8), lead others into sexual immorality (vv. 4, 8), and commit idolatry by denying Jesus Christ (v. 4). They are not slow in imitating Balaam's greed; rather, they rush into (the Greek word ἐκχέω, *ekcheō*, is used for a flooding stream) his error.

they have been destroyed in Korah's rebellion.

They also rebel against authority as Korah and his companions rebelled against Moses and the Lord. Promoting self by resisting authority is characteristic of false teachers (cf. Titus 1:10-11; 2 Timothy 3:1-9; 3 John 9-10). Korah, Dathan, and

Abiram were swallowed by the earth (Numbers 16:32); their followers were destroyed by fire from the Lord (Numbers 16:35). So too, the false teachers of Jude refuse to keep their proper place (like the fallen angels, v. 6), rebel against angels (v. 8) and Jesus (v. 4), and face fiery punishment (v. 7).

All three, Cain, Balaam, and Korah, are examples of rebellion against God's authority. All three destroyed others by their teachings and actions. All three were punished by God. The false teachers in Jude face the same fate.

D. METAPHORS FROM NATURE APPLIED TO THE UNGODLY (12-13)

¹²These men are blemishes at your love feasts, eating with you without the slightest qualm — shepherds who feed only themselves. They are clouds without rain, blown along by the wind; autumn trees, without fruit and uprooted — twice dead. ¹³They are wild waves of the sea, foaming up their shame; wandering stars, for whom blackest darkness has been reserved forever.

v. 12 These men are blemishes at your love feasts,

Jude mines heaven and earth to find six metaphorical examples of the behavior of the false teachers. First, he says they are "blemishes at your love feasts." This is the only place the word "love feast" (ἀγάπη, *agapē*, the plural form here is literally "loves,") is used in the New Testament, although the practice is described by Paul in 1 Corinthians 11:20-22. It is likely that in the first century the Lord's Supper was part of a larger meal, the love feast, where fellowship was expressed, and the poor were fed. Beginning in the second century, the love feast and the Lord's Supper became separated.

The false teachers are "blemishes" or "reefs" (σπίλας, *spilas*, can have either meaning) at the love feasts. If "blemishes" or "spots" is the correct translation (cf. 2 Peter 2:13), then they are like cancers on the body of Christ. However, in keeping with the nature metaphors that follow, "reefs" is a better translation. The false teachers are like dangerous coral reefs that cause others to shipwreck their faith (cf. 1 Timothy 1:19).

eating with you without the slightest qualm — shepherds who feed only themselves.

The irony is clear with either translation. The love feast is to express fellowship with Christ and fellow Christians; these men abuse it by feeding only themselves and eating without reverence for the body of Christ (ἀφόβως, *aphobōs*, "without the slightest qualm," cf. 1 Corinthians 11:29). "Feeding themselves" (literally "shepherding themselves") is a second metaphor, recalling biblical warnings against selfish leaders among God's people (Ezekiel 34:1-10; Isaiah 56:11; John 10:12-13). This language implies the false teachers were fleecing the flock of God by prophesying for profit as Balaam did (v. 11).

They are clouds without rain, blown along by the wind;

Not only are they reefs and evil shepherds, they also are "clouds without rain" (cf. Proverbs 25:14). In a dry climate it is particularly disappointing to expect rain and receive none. So too these false teachers promise much but deliver nothing. "Blown by the wind" indicates their instability (cf. Ephesians 4:14).

autumn trees, without fruit and uprooted — twice dead.

The barrenness of their promises is shown by the fourth metaphor that they are fruitless trees. The figure of fruit for obedience is common in the Bible (cf. Psalm 1:3; John 15:1-6). The Greek word (φθινοπωρινός, *phthinopōrinos*) translated "autumn" is actually "late autumn." Harvest is past, and it is too late for them to produce fruit. "Twice dead" may be a reference to the second death as punishment for the false teachers (cf. Revelation 2:11; 20:6; 21:8). "Uprooted" indicates their separation from the community of the faithful and is also a symbol of punishment (cf. Psalm 52:5; Proverbs 2:22; Jeremiah 1:10; Matthew 3:10; 7:19; 15:13; Luke 13:6-9).

v. 13 They are wild waves of the sea, foaming up their shame;

A fifth metaphor says as waves throw debris up on the seashore, so these men spew forth their shame (cf. Isaiah 57:20). To Israel, the sea was always a symbol of danger and chaos (Psalm 107:23-28; Ezekiel 28:8; Revelation 21:1). Here it is the moral chaos of the false teachers that is the danger.

wandering stars, for whom blackest darkness has been reserved forever.

Finally, they are "wandering stars," perhaps meteors or comets but more likely planets that the ancients thought had irregular courses. Like meteors, the false teachers flash brilliantly for a short time, but they give no lasting light. As the planets wander across the sky, so these men wander from the truth ("wander" [πλανήτης, *planētēs*] is from the same root as "error" in v. 11). "Blackest darkness" reminds one of Jesus' warning of "outer darkness" (Matthew 8:12; 22:13; 25:30).

Taken together, these six metaphors focus on the selfishness ("feeding themselves"), instability ("blown by wind," "wild waves," "wandering stars"), and barrenness ("without rain," "fruitless") of the false teachers. They particularly emphasize the finality of their punishment ("uprooted," "twice dead," "blackest darkness"). Although there are Old Testament parallels, the last four metaphors — clouds, trees, waves, stars — are probably drawn from *The Book of Enoch*, which Jude will quote directly in the next section.

E. ENOCH'S PROPHECY AGAINST THE UNGODLY (14-16)

[14]Enoch, the seventh from Adam, prophesied about these men: "See, the Lord is coming with thousands upon thousands of his holy ones [15]to judge everyone, and to convict all the ungodly of all the ungodly acts they have done in the ungodly way, and of all the harsh words ungodly sinners have spoken against him." [16]These men are grumblers and

faultfinders; they follow their own evil desires; they boast about themselves and flatter others for their own advantage.

v. 14 Enoch, the seventh from Adam, prophesied about these men:

Jude supports his case against the false teachers by quoting from 1 Enoch 1:9 (see the discussion of his use of pseudepigraphical writings in the Introduction), which reads:

> Behold, he will arrive with ten million of the holy ones in order to execute judgment upon all. He will destroy the wicked ones and censure all flesh on account of everything that they have done, that which the sinners and the wicked ones committed against him.[5]

"See, the Lord is coming with thousands upon thousands of his holy ones

Jude adapts the quotation to his circumstances by identifying the one to come with the Lord (that is, Jesus) who will come to judge the ungodly (that is, the false teachers). He comes with an uncountable host (literally myriads) of holy ones, perhaps glorified saints but more likely angels (cf. Deuteronomy 33:2-3; Daniel 7:10; Zechariah 14:5; Matthew 25:31; 2 Thessalonians 1:7; also see the comments on James 5:4). Their holiness contrasts with the ungodliness of the false teachers. The picture here is of a conquering Lord leading his angelic army against the forces of evil.

v. 15 to judge everyone, and to convict all the ungodly of all the ungodly acts they have done in the ungodly way, and of all the harsh words ungodly sinners have spoken against him."

He comes to judge the ungodly (a word used four times in different forms in this single verse). Ungodly (ἀσεβής, *asebēs*) implies both moral fault and rejection of God (that is, of

---

[5]James H. Charlesworth, ed. *The Old Testament Pseudepigrapha* (Garden City: Doubleday, 1983).

Jesus, v. 4). The ungodly will be judged for their acts and harsh words against the Lord Jesus and his angels ("slander celestial beings," v. 8).

v. 16 These men are grumblers and faultfinders; they follow their own evil desires; they boast about themselves and flatter others for their own advantage.

Jude further applies the quotation to his opponents by describing them as grumblers (γογγυσταί, *gongystai*) and faultfinders (μεμψίμοιροι, *mempsimoiroi*). Grumbling against God recalls the Israelites who murmured in the wilderness and were punished by God (v. 5; cf. Exodus 15:24; 16:2, 7-9, 12; Numbers 14:2,27,29,36; Deuteronomy 1:27; Psalm 106:25; 1 Corinthians 10:10) as well as those who rejected the teaching of Jesus (John 6:41). "Faultfinders" is better translated "complainers." Like the fallen angels (v. 6), the false teachers are discontented with the status God has given them, so they grumble and whine.

As an attempt to increase their status, they brag (literally, "speak big" (ὑπέρογκα, *hyperonka*) about themselves and flatter those in power (literally, "admire faces," in other words, judge by appearance, cf. James 2:1-9). Not content to please the Lord Jesus, the all-powerful Lord of hosts, they fawn over those who appear influential but in truth have no permanent power.

F. THE WARNING OF THE APOSTLES (17-19)

¹⁷But, dear friends, remember what the apostles of our Lord Jesus Christ foretold. ¹⁸They said to you, "In the last times there will be scoffers who will follow their own ungodly desires." ¹⁹These are the men who divide you, who follow mere natural instincts and do not have the Spirit.

v. 17 But, dear friends, remember what the apostles of our Lord Jesus Christ foretold.

The address "dear friends" (Greek, "beloved") is a transition, contrasting the false teachers with Jude's readers. Unlike the false teachers who flout authority, the beloved are to hold to the faith once delivered by remembering what they were taught by the apostles, whether personally, through others, or by apostolic writings. Just as the Old Testament (vv. 5-11) and Enoch (vv. 14-15) predicted the coming and fate of the false teachers, so also the apostles foretold their judgment (see Acts 20:29-31; 1 Timothy 4:1-3; 2 Timothy 3:1-9; 4:3; 1 John 2:18-19; 4:1-3). The apostles received this warning from Jesus himself (Mark 13:5-8, 21-23; Matthew 7:15).

v. 18 They said to you, "In the last times there will be scoffers who will follow their own ungodly desires."

The apostolic warning calls the false teachers "scoffers" or "mockers," a word (ἐμπαίκτης, *empaiktēs*) used often in the Old Testament to describe the ungodly (Psalms 1:1; 35:16; Proverbs 1:22; 9:7-8; 13:1; 14:6; 19:25-29). These teachers have scoffed at Christ (vv. 4, 15), at authority (v. 8), at angels (v. 8), and at anything they do not understand (v. 10). Rejecting proper authority, they are left with their own ungodly desires (see v. 16).

v. 19 These are the men who divide you,

These men divide the church, referring not to an actual schism (they still share the same love feasts as the rest of the church, v. 12) but to an attempt to lead others astray (as at Corinth, "I follow Paul," "I follow Apollos," etc. 1 Corinthians 1:10-17). They may have convinced others that they were more enlightened and spiritual than most Christians, and so they deserved to lead the church.

who follow mere natural instincts and do not have the Spirit.

But in his strongest language yet, Jude says they are natural and do not have the Spirit. Paul makes this same contrast between the natural man ("the man without the Spirit," NIV) and the spiritual man (1 Corinthians 2:10-15). James 3:15

speaks of a wisdom that is purely natural or "unspiritual" and so is earthly and of the devil. These false teachers follow their own natural inclinations, and although they may claim dreams and visions from God (v. 8), by their ungodly acts, they show they actually do not have the Spirit. This is the same as saying they have no salvation, since ". . . if anyone does not have the Spirit of Christ, he does not belong to Christ" (Romans 8:9b).

IV. A CALL TO FAITH, LOVE, AND MERCY (20-23)

²⁰But you, dear friends, build yourselves up in your most holy faith and pray in the Holy Spirit. ²¹Keep yourselves in God's love as you wait for the mercy of our Lord Jesus Christ to bring you to eternal life.

²²Be merciful to those who doubt; ²³snatch others from the fire and save them; to others show mercy, mixed with fear — hating even the clothing stained by corrupted flesh.

v. 20 But you, dear friends,

This paragraph begins with a contrast ("But you . . .") and continues to state and imply contrasts between the false teachers and the faithful Christians (the "dear friends," or literally in Greek, "the beloved ones" [ἀγαπητοί, *agapētoi*]). Along with these contrasts are several echoes of previous verses in Jude. Thus, these verses function as a summary.

build yourselves up in your most holy faith

The faithful are encouraged here by a series of four commands. First, they are "to build yourselves up on your most holy faith." The metaphor of the church as a building occurs throughout the New Testament (Matthew 16:18; Acts 20:32; 1 Corinthians 3:9-15; Colossians 2:6-7; and other passages). Here Christians as a group, not just individually, are to build themselves up on faith, that is, on the once-for-all beliefs that were entrusted to them (v. 3). That faith is holy in contrast to the ungodliness of the false teachers. The false teachers are trying to tear down and destroy the faith. The beloved are to build it up.

and pray in the Holy Spirit.

In contrast to the false teachers who do not have the Spirit (v. 19), the faithful are to "pray in the Holy Spirit." This does not necessarily imply charismatic prayer (as in 1 Corinthians 14:13-17), since the Spirit intercedes for Christians whenever they pray (Romans 8:15-16, 26-27; Galatians 4:6; Ephesians 6:18). It is the Spirit who enables us to confess, "Jesus is Lord" (1 Corinthians 12:3; 1 John 4:2), but these false teachers deny Jesus (v. 2) and so cannot pray in the Spirit. Praying in the Spirit means confessing Christ and receiving help in prayer from his Holy Spirit.

v. 21 Keep yourselves in God's love

Thirdly, the faithful are urged to "keep yourselves in God's love." This does not mean "your love for God," but "his love for you." God's love for the Christian is unending, but it calls for effort to stay with the faith and so stay in his love (John 15:9; 1 John 4:16). Unlike the disobedient angels who abandoned their position with God (v. 6), and the false teachers who pervert God's grace and love (v. 4), the beloved ones must be content to remain in God's love where they belong.

as you wait for the mercy of our Lord Jesus Christ to bring you to eternal life.

Finally, Jude encourages them to "wait for the mercy of our Lord Jesus Christ to bring you to eternal life." Although he doesn't use the word, Jude here speaks of the sure hope of the Christian. The beloved have already received mercy (Jude even greets them with the word v. 2), but the mercy of Jesus Christ will be fully revealed at the last day when the saints receive eternal life (cf. 2 Timothy 1:18). Waiting for that day is not merely passive but calls for action — building, praying, and keeping.

In these four injunctions ("build," "pray," "keep," "wait") there are references to the three theological virtues — faith, love, and hope — and to the Trinity — Holy Spirit, God, and Jesus Christ.

v. 22 Be merciful to those who doubt;

The words of verses 22-23 occur in a variety of ways in different Greek manuscripts and English translations.[6] In the NIV there are three classes of people mentioned, each increasingly caught up in the error of the false teachers.

Having strongly condemned the false teachers and their error, the question arises, "How then should we treat those who are tempted to follow their error?" Staying in God's love and waiting for the mercy of Christ motivates the faithful to show love and mercy to others. Some are not sure of what they believe or whom they should follow. Such doubters need mercy, not condemnation. Having mercy on doubters implies the faithful should correct them with gentleness.

v. 23 snatch others from the fire and save them;

Others are in greater danger from the false teachers. They stand on the brink of hellfire. They must be snatched (ἁρπάζω, *harpazō*) from the fire (cf. Zechariah 3:1-5; Amos 4:11) and saved before it is too late (cf. James 5:20). There is a strong sense of urgency here. The faithful cannot ignore those who are tempted to be immoral and to deny Jesus like the false teachers. If ignored, they will suffer the punishment of the ungodly (see vv. 6,7,13,15).

to others show mercy, mixed with fear — hating even the clothing stained by corrupted flesh.

Others are so influenced by the false teachers that it is as if their clothes were soiled by sin (Isaiah 4:4; Zechariah 3:3-4). Such sin can contaminate others, even those who try to show

---

[6]Bruce M. Metzger, *A Textual Commentary on the Greek New Testament* (New York: United Bible Societies, 1971), pp. 727-729.

mercy. False teaching is contagious. Caution or fear is needed to insure that the faithful themselves are not led astray.

These verses clearly show the responsibility that faithful Christians have toward those who are confused about the faith or even living contrary to it. Contending for the faith does not call for treating others harshly. One cannot fight for the faith without having the attitude of the one in whom our faith rests, the one who came to seek and save the lost (Luke 19:10). The faithful are to do all they can in a spirit of gentleness and mercy to restore others to faith, and yet they must be cautious or they too will fall prey to temptation (Galatians 6:1-2).

V. DOXOLOGY (24-25)

²⁴To him who is able to keep you from falling and to present you before his glorious presence without fault and with great joy — ²⁵to the only God our Savior be glory, majesty, power and authority, through Jesus Christ our Lord, before all ages, now and forevermore! Amen.

Jude ends his letter with one of the most beautiful statements of praise in Scripture. This doxology (from δόξα, *doxa*, the Greek word for "glory") is similar to others in the New Testament (Romans 16:25-27; Ephesians 3:20-21; Philippians 4:20; 1 Timothy 1:17; Revelation 5:13) but has unique features that tie it to the rest of Jude.

v. 24 To him who is able to keep you from falling

Jude's praise is to the one "who is able to keep you from falling." The idea of sin as stumbling is found frequently in the Psalms (38:16; 56:13; 66:9; 73:2; 91:12; 116:8; 121:3) and in James (2:10; 3:2). Here stumbling is falling into the error of the false teachers and so suffering the fate of the fallen angels (v. 6). Jude has warned strongly against the danger of being contaminated by false teaching. This warning might have tempted his readers to focus on their own weakness and despair of remaining faithful. Jude moves them to courage by ending his letter with praise for the loving, powerful God who sustains believers. Christians must contend for the faith (v. 3), but they rely on God's strength for the fight, not on their own. Defense ends in praise. As Jude began his letter by calling them "kept by Jesus Christ," so here, using a different Greek word (φυλάσσω, *phylassō*), he ends by praising the God who keeps them.

and to present you before his glorious presence without fault and with great joy —

God will not only keep them from falling now, but he will ultimately allow them to enter his presence without fault and with great joy. Faultless (ἄνωμος, *anōmos*) may imply that they stand before God as unblemished "living sacrifices" (Romans 12:1), just as Old Testament sacrifices were to be without spot or blemish (Exodus 12:5; Leviticus 22:21; Malachi 1:13-14). More likely, it means they will stand morally blameless before God. Christians rejoice in his grace and power that alone can make them blameless (1 Thessalonians 5:23).

v. 25 to the only God our Savior

This God who is able to protect and save is the only God. This reflects the *Shema*, the great Jewish creed that proclaims that the Lord is one (Deuteronomy 6:4; see the comments on James 2:19). It is also a reminder that the false teachers have rejected Jesus as "our only sovereign and Lord" (v. 4), and by doing so have rejected the only God.

God is also "our Savior" (σωτήρ, *sōtēr*), a title usually used for Jesus (but see Luke 1:47; 1 Timothy 1:1; 2:3; 4:10; Titus 1:3; 2:10; 3:4). The term here likely has an Old Testament background, and so is equivalent to the phrase, "the God of our salvation" (Psalms 68:19; 88:1).

be glory, majesty, power and authority, through Jesus Christ our Lord, before all ages, now and forevermore! Amen.

God is praised with four terms. Glory (δόξα, *doxa*) is a rich word pointing to the bright presence of God that overshadowed Sinai (Exodus 24:16-17) and the temple (1 Kings 8:11). It also suggests the reputation and renown of God. Majesty (μεγαλωσύνη, *megalōsynē*) connotes the transcendence of God. He is beyond human comprehension. Power (κράτος, *kratos*) and authority (ἐξουσία, *exousia*) are synonymous. "Authority" may be Jude's final swipe at the false teachers who do not recognize God's rule.

The greatest way to fight false teachers is to praise the God they deny. All praise to God is through Jesus Christ our Lord. That praise stretches from eternity to eternity. To these words of praise, all believers say a heartfelt amen.

APPENDIX

PREACHING AND TEACHING FROM JAMES

This material is adapted from presentations given at the Minister's Sermon Seminar at the Institute for Christian Studies, Austin, Texas, and at the Biblical Preaching Seminar at Lipscomb University, Nashville, Tennessee. Although intended primarily as guides for preaching from James, these suggestions have also been used as source material for topical classes in Bible school settings.

The following repeats in outline form much of what is found in the Introduction to James in the Commentary. The exegetical considerations also reflect the Commentary, but the sermon suggestions are designed to aid application in preaching and teaching.

CONSIDERATIONS ON PREACHING JAMES.

I. What kind of literature is James?
  1. A Letter?
    In form only: Begins as a letter, but no specific audience, setting, or greetings.
  2. Paraenesis.
    Ethical exhortation.
    Similar to Proverbs, Ecclesiasticus, Wisdom of Solomon, 1 Peter, Hermas, and traditional Hellenistic moral instruction.
  3. Challenge of preaching paraenetic material.
    Dangers of moralism and of baptizing conventional wisdom.

4. Lack of central organization. Repeated topics. Lends itself to topical preaching from different passages.

II. Misunderstandings of James.

1. Too Jewish. Emphasizes a works righteousness. Legalistic. No distinctive Christian teaching. "Epistle of Straw" (Luther).

Answer: James' ethic is eschatological. He takes conventional moral wisdom (both Jewish and Greek) and redefines it in light of the incarnation and return of Christ, the end (limit and goal) of time.

2. A Practical Book. Deals with people where they are and answers their questions. Gives concrete steps on how people can improve.

Answer: James is a thoroughly impractical book. He condemns human wisdom. He is pessimistic of human ability, but hopeful of God's transcendent power in the believer. He challenges worldliness in the church with his eschatological perspective.

Exegetical Considerations: James 1:2-4, 12-18; 5:7-12.
Theme: Waiting.

James 1:2-4.

1. "Brothers" (v. 2) used 14 times in James. Pastoral tone. Family implies closeness and responsibility.

2. *All* joy. "All" implies sincerity, not putting best face on trouble. Joy here is not pleasure, but "eschatological anticipated joy" [Davids].

3. "Trials" (v. 2) is an ambiguous word that may refer to trouble, persecution, or temptation (1:12-13). Many kinds ("multicolored") may refer to all three.

4. Trials are also tests (v. 3, see 1 Peter 1:7). Reminds one of Abraham, Job, and others. The effects of trials, not the trials themselves, are described.

5. Tests produce "heroic endurance" (v. 4), steadfastness, fortitude, constancy, strong consistency, staying power.

6. Heroic endurance is not an end in itself, but should be allowed to grow into perfection (a word James uses more often than any N.T. writer). The concern here is for maturity and completeness, not just a static lack of error. Perfection in James is eschatological, that is, brought by God and the end of steadfast obedience (Matthew 5:48).

James 1:12-16.

1. "Blessed" (v. 12) like the Beatitudes (Matthew 5:1-12) with their theme of reversal.

2. "Trial" (v. 12) is the same word as in vv. 3 and 4, and here implies persecution, since temptation should be resisted, not just endured.

3. The crown of life (see Revelation 2:10) refers to escha-

tological blessedness.

4. "Tempted" (v. 13) is the same word as in v. 12, but the context here implies temptation, not testing. God may test, but he does not tempt. We are to blame for our temptations and sins.

5. Desire births sin that grows into death. Contrast with trials that produce endurance that grows into perfection (v. 4). Death vs. the crown of life.

James 5:7-12.

1. Patience (vv. 7,8,10) in this passage is synonymous with endurance (v. 11).

2. "Until the coming" = as you wait for the coming or in light of the coming.

3. Early and late rain (v. 7) perhaps implies waiting for the Lord's current and future coming.

4. Do not grumble (v. 9). Patience is not just waiting for the Lord, but also bearing with others.

5. "Blessed" (v. 11) ties this passage with James 1:12-18.

6. Job may seem a strange example of patience, since he was bold enough to blame God for his troubles. However, he did show heroic endurance (better than "patience") by maintaining his relation to God and calling on God to appear.

Preaching Challenge: Preaching to an age of activity.

**Homiletic Suggestion: "Those Who Stand and Wait":
Preaching Text: James 1:12-18.**

Introduction: We live in an age where activity is prized. We feel ashamed if we are not overworked. In the church, activity is usually given as the solution to our problems: "We need to be excited, on fire, out doing for the Lord." To stand by and wait for something to happen is thought to show a lack of devotion. But at times of illness when we cannot work, or times of reflection when we are thinking straight, we realize that God does not need our efforts.

In reflecting on his own inability to serve, John Milton in his sonnet "On His Blindness" reminds us:
"God doth not need
 Either man's work or his own gifts. Who best
Bear his mild yoke, they serve him best. His state
 Is kingly: thousands at his bidding speed,
And post o'er land and ocean without rest;
 They also serve who only stand and wait."

I. Stand the Test of Pain and Persecution. (James 1:2-4; 5:10-11).

We may not be persecuted, but we still face "multi-colored trials": pain, sickness, grief, and doubt. What should we do in the face of trials? Not look for easy solutions, but grit our teeth and stand the pain. Like Job, we face trials not with a false, accepting "patience," but with heroic endurance, refusing to break relation with God.

II. Wait For Endurance to Produce Character. (James 1:2-4). Heroic endurance is not an end in itself; by standing the pain of trials, we are being transformed, even perfected by God. Standing the test produces a character of maturity.

III. Stand Against Temptation. (James 1:12-16). Temptation comes not from God, but from our own desires. We cannot get off the hook for temptation and sin. Instead of rationalizing our behavior by blaming others (God, Satan, family, society), we should fight temptation with the help of God. Here standing is not heroic endurance, but an active war against sin.

IV. Wait for the Coming of the Lord. (James 5:7-8). This is more than "pie in the sky," or "farther along we'll know more about it." The Lord comes in the present as well as the future. As the farmer stands and waits for rain, so we wait for Christ to act. But Christ's timetable may not be ours. We need patience. Waiting for Christ to act is a long process; it may take our whole life. But our whole existence as Christians is based on our confidence that he will come, that he will act on our behalf. Our task is to stand and wait.

Exegetical Considerations: James 1:5-8; 3:13-18.
Theme: Wisdom.

James 1:5-8.

1. Setting: after section on trial and endurance.
2. To lack nothing (v. 4) is the goal of endurance, but if one lacks wisdom, one should ask God for it.
3. Wisdom reminds one of O.T. parallels, particularly the Wisdom books of Proverbs, Ecclesiastes, and Job.
4. God gives "generously" (the word is found only here in the N.T.), which is better translated "straightforwardly" (with no strings attached) or without hesitation (contrast with "double-minded").
5. He also gives ungrudgingly or "without insult." Thus God is no reluctant, critical Giver.
6. So wisdom here is a gift of grace, unlike O.T. wisdom which can to some extent be "searched out."
7. James 1:6-8 will be discussed in a later sermon on prayer.

James 3:13-18.

1. Wisdom is displayed by good deeds and meekness.
2. True wisdom is contrasted with jealousy or rivalry and with a party spirit or selfish ambition or greedy politics or self-promotion. This second wisdom is not heavenly, but progresses from earthly to sensual (unspiritual) to demonic. It leads to all kinds of wickedness. James' readers ". . . have not traded in worldly views of power for God's viewpoint" (Perkins).
3. Verse 17 is a list of virtues, called "the fruit of righteousness," similar to other N.T. passages. Particularly "fruit" reminds one of Galatians 5:22-23. J.A. Kirk (*NT*

Studies 16 [1969], 24-38), suggests that in James wisdom functions as the Holy Spirit does in the rest of the N.T.

Preaching challenge: Preaching against "what everyone knows" to be true.

Homiletic Suggestion: Uncommon Sense.
Preaching Text: James 1:5-8; 3:13-18.
Introduction:
What does it take to be a winner, achieve excellence, or find happiness in the world? What passes for common sense today (as shaped by entertainment, self-help books, and success seminars) tells us that positive thinking, self-promotion, and tapping into hidden internal resources ("the inner child") will bring us happiness. Is this true or is there a better way?

I. James talks of an earthly wisdom or "common sense" that is based in ambition and self-promotion (3:14). Such wisdom is not only earthly, but unspiritual and even demonic. It promises much, but leads to all sorts of evil (3:16).

II. In contrast, there is a wisdom from above that produces good behavior and true happiness and success. This wisdom expresses itself in purity, peace, gentleness, mercy, and a willingness to yield to others (a sharp contrast to self-promotion, 3:17).

III. Great courage is called for to reject the first type of common sense. To even question the value of ambition and self-promotion marks one as strange and perhaps even irrational in the eyes of most. Some may call us lazy, critical, or even unAmerican. Still we must stand firm against such a view.

IV. But how in the world can one achieve the second kind of wisdom, if it is so foreign to natural common sense? How can we, on our own, catch the vision of happiness and success this vision promises? We cannot. Not on our own. This wisdom is from above (3:15, 17). It is a gift of God that comes only through faithful prayer (1:5-8).

V. Do you lack wisdom? Are you caught in the "common sense" of this age? Then ask God and he will generously and gladly give.

Exegetical Considerations: James 1:9-11; 2:1-13; 5:1-6. Theme: Rich and poor.

James 1:9-11.

1. The great reversal of rich and poor is a theme found in the O.T. and the N.T. (particularly Luke). There are also echoes here of the Beatitudes. The "humiliation" of the rich is not an inner feeling, but a transformation (reversal) in status.

2. "Grass" is a popular Jewish image of the transitoriness of life (See Isaiah 40:6-8).

3. "In the midst of pursuits" may be translated "in the middle of his travels." James may have traveling merchants in mind.

James 2:1-13.

1. 2:1-4 is a diatribe against partiality, literally "judging by the face."

2. Verses 2-4 provide a hypothetical example (diatribes have theoretical sparring partners) with a sharp, stylized contrast between rich and poor.

3. Two asides: Does the use of the term "synagogue" for a Christian assembly imply a Jewish context for James? Is the setting here worship or a legal assembly?

4. Verse 4 is difficult to translate, but probably means "Have you not made distinctions among yourselves?"

5. Verses 5-13 is a homily against partiality. The move is from the specific to the general: generally the rich have oppressed the poor and opposed Christ. By contrast, the poor have a special place in God's heart: they are chosen to inherit his riches (a prominent O.T. theme, particularly in the Psalms).

6. Partiality or prejudice may seem a minor sin, a mere human foible, but it is a sin against love of neighbor (the royal law) and as such is as bad as adultery or murder (compare Matthew 5:21-26).

7. This entire section is parallel to Matthew 7:1-14.

James 5:1-6.

1. Again the rich are generally unrighteous. Their riches will not last ("rust" in Matthew 6:19-21) and will even testify against them (cf. "treasure" in Matthew 6:19).

2. The poor cry to the Lord of Hosts (a term of power and vengeance) for vindication (compare Abel's blood and Deuteronomy 24:14ff.) "Fattened for slaughter," see Jeremiah 12:13.

SUMMARY: In James the poor are always righteous and the rich are always evil. This is a generalization and is not always true. However, we should resist the temptation to spiritualize these passages by making "poor" merely a term for the community of the faithful. James's warning is clear: riches are to be viewed not as a sign of grace or a benign blessing, but as at best a snare and a temptation and at worst a sign of judgment.

Preaching challenge: Preaching to people who see themselves as neither rich, nor poor.

Homiletic Suggestion: Face Value.
Preaching Text: James 2:1-13.
Introduction:

What kind of people does it take to build a stable church? At face value, it would seem a church of affluent professional people would provide the kind of social and financial stability a church needs. Given a choice, would we not prefer to have well-off church members, instead of those on the brink of poverty?

Wouldn't such a church be more successful?

I. James calls this preference for the rich "favoritism" or "partiality" and he condemns it in no uncertain terms. To prefer the rich makes us ungodly judges who violate the royal law, a sin as bad as adultery or murder (James 2:1-13).

II. Is not James himself partial to the poor? In a sense, yes. He does not say "never judge between rich and poor," but rather gives new standards for judgment. The gospel turns our values upside down.

The rich will lose their riches (1:9-11). Their wealth will count against them in judgment, because they have lived in luxury, cheated the workers, blasphemed Christ (2:7), and even murdered the righteous (5:1-6).

The poor by contrast have been chosen to be rich in faith and inherit the kingdom.

III. As we saw in the last sermon, "common sense" will not always work as a biblical standard for church building. James calls for conversion, for reversing our standards. If the church should target anyone, it should reach out with good news to the poor. Perhaps one reason our churches have failed to grow is that we try to build churches on those who are self-sufficient, instead of on those in need.

Exegetical Considerations: James 1:19,26; 3:1-12.
Theme: The Tongue.

James 1:19-20.
This passage may be against hasty utterances generally, or against setting oneself up as a teacher (thus "slow to speak" the word of God, vv. 18,22).

James 1:26-27.
"Claims to be religious" may again refer to religious teachers. If the teacher does not bridle the tongue (a phrase used only in James in the N.T.), he deceives himself. Religious talk is no good without action to back it up.

James 3:1-12.
1. Teachers were important leaders in the early church (1 Corinthians 12:28; Acts 13:1; Romans 12:7; Ephesians 4:11). One desiring the authority and prestige of a teacher should also beware of the strict judgment (or harsher penalties) they face, stricter because of their influence and understanding. Those who teach are accountable for those who are taught (1 Corinthians 3:10-15).
2. Verses 2-12 is a traditional diatribe against the tongue. James draws from Jewish sources (Proverbs) and from Hellenistic moral thought and literature. Examples: "bridle" — Sophocles; "rudder" — Aristotle, Plutarch, Philo; "fire" — Proverbs 16:27, Sirach 28:22, Greek moralists; "fig" — Epictetus.
3. Verse 6, "stains the whole body," contrast with pure "unstained" religion (1:27).

4. Verses 9-12, the tongue's "doubleness" is one of James' pet peeves. Compare the double-minded man (1:7-8), and the one who says, but does not do (2:14-17).

Preaching challenge: Avoiding a legalistic morality on one hand and "cheap grace" on the other by calling for a change of heart.

Homiletic Suggestion: We Need Fewer Teachers.
Preaching Text: James 3:1-12.
Introduction.

We need fewer teachers! Such an announcement has probably never been made in our churches. Usually we must beat the bushes for teachers. If you've ever been in charge of recruiting teachers for Bible school, you know how difficult it can be.

I. Yet James says clearly, "Not many of you should become teachers." Why would one not want to be a teacher? There is authority, prestige, and honor in the role. We all like to be experts. But a great responsibility is on the shoulder of a teacher. He can influence for good or evil. Thus he faces stricter judgment and harsher penalties. Why is the teacher in such a dangerous position? Because he uses the uncontrollable tongue.

II. But what if you're not a teacher and don't plan to be? Can you relax and let this sermon pass you by? No. Because even if you do not teach, you have a tongue. Your small tongue rules your body as a bridle rules a horse or a rudder rules a ship. It is an out-of-control fire that cannot be tamed.

III. What sins are committed by the tongue? Anger (1:19), slander (4:11), swearing (5:12), and inconsistency (3:9-12). To James, the last is the worst. One must not praise God and then curse his brother or sister.

IV. So what do we do with our tongues? At one level, the answer is clear: "be slow to speak," watch what you say, think before you speak, work on controlling your tongue. But if the tongue is untamable, why try? Because God can tame it and us. What is at stake here is not just watching your words, but being controlled by God. It's not so much about self-improvement, but about character.

V. So, whether we teach or not, the real question is "Who controls our speech?" or rather "Who controls our life?" The answer to this question is seen not in our intention, but in our speech and actions.

Exegetical Considerations: James 5:13-19.
Theme: Prayer.

1. Verses 13-16 is a saying dealing with various life situations; these are introduced not by conditional clauses (If . . . Then), but as independent sentences (One is . . . Let him), perhaps implying the universality of suffering, cheerfulness, and sickness. Sickness is particularly singled out.

2. Oil here has been understood as medicinal, ceremonial (as in an exorcism), or symbolic of prayer. The reference here is to healing through the miraculous power of Jesus ("in the name of the Lord"), however, v. 15 ascribes this power not to the elders themselves, but to the prayer of faith.

3. The prayer of faith will "save" the sick and the Lord will "raise them up." These terms refer to both cure and resurrection.

4. Verse 15b introduces forgiveness of sins. Here sin is associated with illness. Verse 16 continues the themes of sin, confession, and intercession, and introduces Elijah as an example of one who prays righteously and effectively.

5. Verses 19-20 are a commentary on the admonition in v. 16 to "pray for one another."

Sermon challenge: Preaching to people who believe in "providence," not the power of God through prayer.

Homiletic Suggestion: Pain, Pleasure, Sickness, Sin.
Preaching Text: James 5:13-19.

I. Some of us are hurting. It may be the pain of grief, the agony of defeat and failure, the ache of depression, the strain of worry, or the frustration of life in general. Our pain is real and must not be denied. What do we do when we are in pain? We pray.

II. Some of us are happy. Ecstatic. All goes well with us. We had a week of triumph and accomplishment. We feel good. How do we express our joy? We sing. We sing praise to the God who gives us blessings.

III. Some of us are sick. Some have minor, but nagging illnesses. Some face life-threatening disease. What do we do? We ask for prayer. We ask spiritual leaders to pray for us. Yet it is not the elders or the oil that heals; it is God who hears the prayer of faith and who saves and raises us.

We are not here promised healing from all disease, but we should be bold enough to ask. God is a good and generous God. He can and he will heal. Yet his will is greater than ours. If he does not save us now and raise us from the sick bed, he will save and raise us from the grave.

IV. Some of us are sinful. Some? Don't you mean all? Well, yes and no. All sin. No one has perfect spiritual health, just as no one has perfect physical health. Yet just as some are sick enough to need special help, so too some of us are spiritually sick, caught in a sin and unable to get out. What should we do? Confess our sins to one another. Pray for one another. God will forgive, and heal, and save our soul from death.

Conclusion:

Prayer is for all situations of life: joy and sorrow, pain and pleasure, health and sickness, righteousness and sin. Prayer is effective when nothing else is. It can stop or bring the rain. It can heal, and save, and raise up. Faithful prayer is effective, not because of the way it makes us feel, but because of the God to whom we pray.

Exegetical Considerations: James 1:6-8; 4:1-10.
Theme: Prayer.

James 1:6-8.

1. Faith is connected with the granting of prayer requests in many N.T. passages (Mark 2:5; 4:40; 5:34, 36; 9:23f.; 11:23f.; Matthew 8:10; 9:28; Romans 4:20-21). In v. 6, faith is not a general term, but refers to the certainty that the request will be fulfilled.

2. The sea metaphor (v. 6) is common in ancient literature.

3. Double-minded is a term for indecision, doubt, and unbelief. Specifically here it is doubt that God will grant wisdom. Such a person is unsettled and unstable in faith. Double-minded may be contrasted with loving God with all your heart.

James 4:1-10.

1. "Wars and conflicts" refers to church fights. These spring not from defense of truth, but from desires or cravings (*hedonai*, a different word than in 1:14-15) that fight in our members (probably referring to our individual bodies, not church members).

2. Murder (v. 2) does not seem to fit the context. Some (beginning with Erasmus) have suggested the text was originally "you are jealous," but there is no textual evidence for this reading. Desire leading to murder is not an unbelievable concept (Cain and Abel, Matthew 5:21ff., 1 John 3:15).

3. Unmade prayers will not be answered, but selfish prayer will also not be answered.

4. Verses 4-6 condemn such prayers as examples of double-

mindedness, pride and hypocrisy (the attempt to befriend God and the world). Such selfishness is apostasy ("Adulterers!").

5. Verses 7-10 call for repentance. Note the descriptions of repentance: submit, draw near, cleanse, purify, lament, mourn, weep, humble. Only such repentance can allow God to restore relationship ("he will exalt you"), including prayer.

Challenge: Preaching to those who separate prayer and life.

Homiletic Suggestion: How Not to Pray.
Preaching Text: James 4:1-10.

Introduction.

How often do we pray? Most will answer "not often enough." When do you pray? Regularly, only when we think of it, only when you're in trouble? Many of us neglect our prayer life and feel guilty for doing so. But if we fail to pray, we are not only guilty, but foolish. God wants to give and we will not ask! But God is not just concerned with how often we pray; he also cares how we pray. This is why James warns us how not to pray.

I. Don't forget to pray! (4:2). "You do not have because you do not ask." How often do we rely on our own power instead of God's? We do not pray because we think we can handle things ourselves, or conversely, because we think our request is too great even for God. We don't pray for headaches (we take aspirin), but we don't pray for the terminally ill (there's no hope for him).

II. Don't pray with selfish desires! (4:1-3). First, don't pray against a brother (4:1-2). Church fights are usually based on personalities, not principles. We insist on our own way, but we dare not ask God to give us our will, but his. Secondly, don't ask for gifts that are purely selfish, that will not benefit others.

III. Don't pray with worldly motives! (4:4-10). "Worldly" conjures up pictures of "don't dance, drink, smoke" sermons. What James condemns is "trying to have it all." We cannot have it all. We cannot be a friend of the world, enjoy its wealth, status and power, and also be a friend of God. We cannot pray for success and faithfulness. Repentance and humility are needed to restore relation to God.

IV. Don't doubt God's goodness in prayer! (1:6-8). Do we sometimes pray thinking, "I hope God does this for me," but deep down we think he won't? James calls this being "double-minded." We believe, but we don't. Like a storm-tossed ship, we go back and forth in our faith. True, at times we do not know God's will for us. But we know he wants to give us wisdom and other spiritual gifts. For those we can (and must) pray with no doubts, believing in the goodness and power of our God.

Conclusion:

How to pray: Continually, with concern for others, humbly, in a relationship with God, with full assurance of faith.

Exegetical Considerations: James 1:22-27; 2:14-26.
Theme: Faith as active obedience.

James 1:22-27.
1. The heart of this passage is the mirror analogy: one who looks in a mirror, sees the need for improvement, but doesn't change is like the one who hears, but doesn't act. One who looks into the law of liberty (a significant term for James's understanding of morality) is called to a new character, one requiring perseverance in action. "Mirror" may also refer to an ideal image of moral exempla [Plutarch].
2. "Doing" is given concrete meaning in self-control and compassion for those in need. Widows and orphans, see Exodus 22:22; Deuteronomy 10:18; Psalm 68:5; Isaiah 1:10-17; Jeremiah 5:8.
3. Mere hearers practice self-deception. They are convinced they have true religion because they have heard the words of salvation.

James 2:14-26.
1. Note that James says "you say you have faith" (v. 14). Such "faith" can only be claimed, not shown.
2. Good intentions and warm feelings do no practical good, and so are not true faith (2:15-16).
3. Examples:
   "Faith" without works: demons (who can recite the *Shema*, Deuteronomy 6:4) v. 19; a dead body, v. 26.
   Faith shown by works: Abraham, vv. 21-24; Rahab, v. 25. Both show faith by works of hospitality.
4. James would agree with Paul that Abraham was justified by faith, but not by merely a spoken or claimed

faith, but by a tested faith. Paul also uses the language of "working faith" (see 1 Thessalonians 1:3; 2 Thessalonians 1:11).

5. James may be fighting the idea that salvation by faith is purely personal and does not require obligation to others. He too, like us, may have known uninvolved church members.

Preaching Challenge: Preaching to people who have left legalism for an easy "faith" that does not demand obedience.

**Homiletic Suggestion: Preaching What You Practice.
Preaching Text: James 2:14-26.**

Introduction: What makes one a Christian? What gives true religion?

I. Going to church? (James 1:22-25). If you're 50 years old, have gone to church all your life, four services per week, then you've heard over 10,000 sermons and Bible lessons in your life. 10,000!

So, are you truly religious? Most would say, "You bet." Most would call you a religious nut (10,000 lessons!). But Christianity is not a spectator sport. Hearing and knowing are no good unless acted upon.

If you look in a mirror and see a smudge on your face, it does you no good if you walk away and forget. So too, if you go to church and see yourself in the perfect law of freedom and do nothing to change, it does you no good.

II. Do good intentions make one religious? (James 1:27; 2:14-17). We are all nice people here who wouldn't hurt a fly and who feel strongly for those in need. But if I'm hungry, it does me no good to know you have warm feelings for me. I need food. Intending to do right and even feeling compassion do no good unless they result in action.

III. Faith makes one a Christian. Surely that is true; we have many Scriptures that prove that's true. But what is faith? Believing in the one God? Demons do that. Is it talking the right talk? Confessing Christ? Claiming faith? No, faith is an active verb, it's something you do.

But wasn't Abraham made right by faith (Romans

4:3)? Surely all we have to do to be like him is to confess, "Yes, I believe." But Abraham did his faith; he put it into action by offering Isaac. His faith was not faith until tested.

Faith includes caring for those in need. It implies obligation.

Conclusion:

We often talk of practicing what we preach, as if Christianity was a verbal message that must be acted upon. But Christian faith is first of all something that is done. The gospel is the message of what God has done. Faith is our response to his action in Christ. Christianity is a life, not a recitation of doctrine. Teaching follows the life of faith. We preach what we practice.